ZOOM

Bundle 2 books in 1.

Everything You Need to Know for Teaching with
Zoom Even if You Are a Complete Beginner.
A Complete Step by Step Guide + Bonus 50 Tips
for The Effective Online Teacher

ANDREW MURCEY

THIS BOOK INCLUDES

BOOK 1:

ZOOM FOR BEGINNERS

Everything You Need to Know About Using Zoom for Meetings, Teaching and Videoconferences. Easy to Read with Useful Tips to Perform Professionally on Video

BOOK 2:

TEACHING WITH ZOOM:

A Step-by-Step Beginners Guide to Zoom, The Essential Software Worldwide for Teaching and Learning Online. Bonus: 50 Tips for The Effective Online Teacher.

ZOOM FOR BEGINNERS

Table of Contents

TEACHING WITH ZOOM:

Table of Contents

ZOOM FOR

BEGINNERS

Everything You Need to Know About Using Zoom

for Meetings, Teaching and Videoconferences.

Easy to Read with Useful Tips to

Perform Professionally on Video

ANDREW MURCEY

Introduction

Zoom has features that can help you to organize a meeting formally. Zoom is the best tool for online teaching as it gives whiteboard, annotation, screen sharing, keyboard shortcuts, and much more. Scheduling, joining, starting a conference, and sending invitations to your participants for a video conference is easy with Zoom. It has an assignment and presentations set up as a tool for instructors to involve students in a better learning process. For feedback, there is a polling feature to create a poll and share it with your participants. If you are looking for an application for your meetings and video/audio conferences, try out Zoom as it will provide you with the best features as compared to other tools, including price plans.

Zoom Video Communications is an independent information service located in California. It provides video telecommunications and online messaging services through a peer-to-peer software system based in the cloud. It is used for video conferencing, working from home, distance learning, and social connections. Zoom's corporate model relies on delivering a product that is easy to use than alternatives, as well as cost advantages, which involves reducing infrastructure-level hardware expenses and ensuring a strong degree of workforce productivity. It supports video chatting service, which allows unlimited access to up to a hundred devices at once, with a time limit of forty minutes for free accounts having meetings with five or more members.

Customers have the opportunity to update any subscription to one of their plans, with the maximum allowing up to a thousand persons simultaneously, with no time limit. With the emergence of remote working in this scenario, Zoom's software utilization has seen a significant global rise starting in early 2020. Its software applications have been subject to review by the public and media concerning privacy and security issues. A portion of the Zoom working population is based in China that has given rise to concerns about monitoring and censorship. Business conferencing apps such as Zoom Rooms are accessible for fifty to one hundred dollars a month. One screen can display up to forty-nine users at once. Zoom has several levels: Basic, Pro, Enterprise, and Business. If you are using Mozilla Firefox or Google Chrome, participants do not have to download the app; they can click on the link and enter from the web page. For Macs, this is not the case with Safari.

Banking institutions, universities, and other educational departments around the globe use Zoom. Zoom has a record of ten million regular customers, and the app had more than two hundred million active users in March 2020, generating expanded difficulties for the business. The company launched version 5.0 of Zoom in April which resolved a range of privacy and security issues.

CHAPTER 1:

Why Choose Zoom?

Zoom Cloud Meetings is a web platform that is used to give live, remote lessons. The teacher, from their home, holds a videoconference, a remote lesson that all students can access at the same time, from any device they have. Provided, of course, that it is connected to the Internet. During the lesson everyone sees their teacher, and, in smaller boxes, their classmates connected. The teacher can show cards or exercises for the pupils on the screen.

Zoom is not that difficult to use and it is a free platform that you can access the lessons even without registering.

Zoom is therefore a cloud-based videoconferencing service that you can use to virtually meet other people, either on video or just audio or both, and allows you to record those sessions for later viewing. It provides several tools to respond to many uses.

The Zoom Room is an ideal environment to organize video conferences with high-quality audio and video. It offers the possibility to record and transcribe all the video chat. The Zoom Phone is the function to make simple voice-only calls using data traffic or LAN/Wi-Fi network. Additionally, Screen Share is the function that allows you to share the screen with other participants.

Webinar Zoom offers all the main functions to organize a training webinar that you can broadcast on Facebook or YouTube and thus organize your social webinars. You can share your space with 100 other users and allow viewing at 10,000 sessions without interactions, except with the permission of the organizer.

Right now, most workers are operating right now from home because of the current scenario all over the world. Teamwork right now is incredibly challenging. Software solutions such as Zoom, however, help you communicate. You might use Zoom to hold a community meeting with all of your staff regardless of where each participant is. Additionally, you can hold one-on-one meetings, workshops for employee training, and more through the Zoom website. Such critical technologies make it easier for management practitioners to link and involve their diverse teams, and keep their businesses going productively forward.

Zoom has several useful functionality tools. Yet fortunately, because of the elegant Zoom design, these functions are simple to use. Many of the features of the video conferencing system are readily available and need limited instruction to allow full use of them. When you want to get lost, the Zoom page provides loads of support tools. Finally, Zoom is helpful because it does not charge you to use your corporation. It is pretty cheap in fact regarding the abundance of characteristics it comes with. You can use functions for free though Zoom still provides premium plans with comprehensive feature sets. But even these will not make any difference, ensuring good return on investment for the organizations that use it.

REMOTE WORKING

We are trying to maintain things stable while the condition are challenging - particularly during global a crises. One such thing is to change roles and work from home while we are used to going to the workplace every day. In these days of video calling, tweeting, and file sharing, remote work has been a part of the daily lifestyle of many cultures for years, and although the transition may seem challenging, it is not impossible.

Developers take on our staff's technology strategies, and the knowledge of many of our reporters and editors, to put together information and suggestions on working from home. This involves both detailed information about working remotely, having to deal with conference calls, and make a decent standing desk, but also quick tips on how to utilize Zoom. Zoom can help in organizing class meetings and staff meetings sitting at home. It can help you to work remotely no matter where you are and what you are doing.

WORK FROM HOME

Remote job and teaching more effective are becoming increasingly common in schools and businesses around the globe, and institutions need to ensure their employees have the techniques they need to get the best communications experience at home. Zoom is introducing the unveiling of the latest category, Zoom for Home, as part of our commitment to helping anyone operating from home, which enables you to access a dedicated personal communication tool for video presentations, phone calls, and immersive whiteboard.

Each group incorporates updates to the Zoom app with compatible equipment for improving the home business experience.

Zoom for Home is also compliant with all Zoom Rooms Devices, like Sleek and Poly hardware options, enabling consumers to pick the equipment they need to build the ideal work-from, home connectivity experience through spaces including the family room.

Sign in to a computer compliant with Zoom for Home with a Zoom user profile to immediately create interactive office environments with no additional licenses (Zoom for Home is eligible for all Zoom discussion licenses, except Basic).

- Easily schedule meetings, work collaboratively virtually with information sharing and annotation and send and receive telephone calls.
- Synchronizes with the user's schedule, status, conference settings, and phone for an embedded video-first identity management experience.

Zoom for home computers may be established for virtual IT control through the admin app, or end-user self-service. This ensures the equipment is primarily developed for simple operation with minimal or no IT assistance is suited for desk configurations and matches the price level for setting up a home workplace.

A CHANCE TO WORK ON YOUR PASSION

If you should do one thing to change your life, it is doing what you are excited about and using it as a profession, as a career, or as a passion. While this is not easy, the path is worth it because it pays off when you are doing something that you enjoy.

It is not easy to work on your passion while attending a hectic routine. A tiring job or a student routine can make you keep your passion aside. During the current scenario, there is a lot of time for everyone to take a stand and work hard on passion while staying at home using Zoom. It can help you to learn additional things and taking classes in different short courses. Zoom provides excellent benefits for its users, especially in the learning process.

GOOD FOR ONLINE TEACHING

As a teacher, if you or your learners have a situation that keeps you from meeting the person, Zoom can help maintain your class going. Online class meetings, in which everyone is planned to join a Zoom meeting, are one way to create interaction when learners are remote, but Zoom can also be used to assist other learning and teaching situations. So long as a student attendant is on a laptop, they can select a connection to the URL and be taken to a chat with the instructor instantly. This removes slow updates entirely, annoying bonus services, and plenty of boring things. Often people need to upgrade their software or flash to reach, but that never transforms into an issue that lasts more than two minutes. It is suitable for first-time gatherings and already-off meetings. Zoom provides different beneficial features for online classes like a whiteboard, screen sharing, screen recording, assignment and presentation setup, etc.

CHAPTER 2:

Getting Started, Downloading and Setting Up

GET STARTED WITH ZOOM

B efore we learn about accessing and starting Zoom Meetings, the best way to learn about it is through downloading and installing the Zoom app. This will simplify its accessibility factor. Whether you are hosting a meeting or attending as a participant, using Zoom can be extremely effortless once you follow these steps.

DOWNLOAD THE APP:

If you are using your computer or laptop, you will see this window below as soon as you enter.

Upon using a mobile app, an interface like this will pop up as soon as you enter.

For easier understanding, we are assuming that you are using the desktop version of Zoom.

START A NEW MEETING

If you are hosting a meeting, click on the 'New Meeting' option that is represented by the orange icon. You will enter an interface that enables you to change the settings according to your preferences.

AUDIO SETTINGS

First, you will tweak the audio settings. To begin with, find the 'Join Audio' at the bottom-left corner of the window and click the arrow beside it. Click on 'Audio Settings' from the dropdown menu. A 'Settings' window will pop up, which will look like this.

You can always access this window by clicking on the setting icon on the top right part of the screen

Once the window pops up, click on the dropdown list located on the right side of 'Test Speaker' and select the speaker you prefer. You can either choose your headphone jack, your device's speaker, or any other speaker that is linked externally. We would recommend that you wear headphones as it will block out background noise and keep your meeting private if other people are around.

Next, you should check the microphone quality. Click on the dropdown menu on the right side of 'Test Mic.' Depending on the microphone device you are using, select the relevant option.

If you have an external microphone connected to your system, the list will display the name. If not, select 'same as a system' to use the device's microphone.

Then, you will check the input level of your microphone and voice quality.

Start talking and view the slider besides 'Input Level' as it transitions from red to green.

Your audio is stable if you are in the green zone (not too slow and not too loud). Check the box beside 'Automatically adjust microphone volume' to make it easier.

Leave the other settings as they are. You can probably check the box that says 'Join audio by computer when joining a meeting' to access the same setup as soon as you join a call.

CHAT OPTIONS

You can access the 'Chat' option on the bottom of the main window. It will open a popup window. This will allow you to write comments and send messages during the meeting.

You can also upload files or photos from your device, Google Drive, or Dropbox by clicking on the file icon.

This is particularly convenient if you want to discuss certain specifications during the meeting, such as presentations, reports, or diagrams. In case you wish to send a private message to a participant you will need to click on "everyone" and select from the list the person that you wish to contact.

END THE MEETING

To end the meeting or the exit, select 'End Meeting,' denoted in red in the bottom-right corner. Select 'End Meeting for All' from the pop-up window to end the meeting.

SCHEDULE A MEETING

Now let's try scheduling the next meeting, go to the main page of your app, and click on the icon that says 'Schedule.'
You will see a window like this.

Type the name of the subject, class, or topic of discussion of the meeting in the 'Topic' box. Select the starting and ending date and time of the meeting. Since we are learning the features on the free version of Zoom, you can set only 40 minutes. To increase the duration, go to the official website and buy a subscription plan that offers longer meetings and additional benefits.

Next, select the box beside 'Generate Automatically' under 'Meeting ID' (this should be your preferred option).

Then, generate a password by checking the box beside the 'Require meeting password.' Type a password of your choosing and share it with the other participants to give them access to the meeting. By unchecking the box, anyone can access the meeting without a password, so, it's always preferable to create a password.

Next, you can select whether you want your video to be on or off during the meeting. You also have the option to choose whether you want your participants' video to be on or off.

For the audio, select 'Telephone and Computer Audio,' as some of your participants might use their phone and cellular data if they don't have a stable broadband connection.

You can add this schedule reminder on a calendar of your choice. Choose among iCal, Google Calendar, or any other calendar that you use.

Lastly, click on Advanced Options and select your preferred option among 'Enable waiting room' (lets your participants wait before starting the meeting), 'Enable join before host' (lets your participants enter the meeting before you do), 'Mute participants on entry' (mutes all participants until you enter and unmute), and 'Record the meeting automatically on the local computer' (begins recording without selecting the option).

Once you select the appropriate options, click on 'Schedule' and your meeting will be noted on your calendar. When you open your calendar, you will receive the details regarding the meeting, including the meeting ID, password, and even a mobile tap feature that takes you to the meeting directly if accessed through a cell phone. Send this auto-generated message containing the meeting details to your desired participants through e-mail or text.

HOME PAGE OPTIONS

A few more options that can be accessed from the home page (located on the top of the page) include:

Chat: If you have made a few friends on Zoom and added them, they will appear on this Chat on a panel. You can directly chat with them through this option.

Meetings: With this option, you can check all the meetings that you have scheduled for a future date or the ones that have been scheduled for you by someone else. The panel will also show your Meeting ID or PMI. With your PMI, you can use options such as Copy Invitation, Edit, or Join from a Room.

Contacts: You can view your added contacts in this panel, both from your directory and channels.

Your profile: You can change your profile settings by selecting your picture icon on the top-right corner of the home page. This is your avatar. You can add a personal note, set your status as Away, Available, or Do Not Disturb (you can choose the duration), make changes to your profile, and upgrade to the Pro version.

AS A PARTICIPANT

Follow *"Start a new meeting"* as mentioned above.

Tweak the audio, video, and recording settings as explained above.

To join a particular meeting, you can either copy and paste the given URL into your browser, or enter the meeting password after logging in. A password is a 9-digit number that is generated when a host creates a meeting.

If you have the meeting URL, go to your web browser, paste the URL, and press Enter. If you have already downloaded the Zoom app, you will be asked if you want to be directed to Zoom. If not, it will open the window in your browser.

Once you press Enter, you will see something like this.

If you have the meeting password, log in to Zoom or open the Zoom app, and click on 'Join.' Type in your meeting password and your name. Click on Join.

Use 'Mute/Unmute' or 'Start/Stop Video' at the bottom of the screen as you wish. If you swipe left, you will have an option that says 'Tap to Speak' in the center of the screen. Tap on the circle when you want to speak and release it to mute it automatically.

To chat, update Meeting Settings, change the background, or to raise your hand to speak, tap on 'More' in the bottom-right corner. Select the option you want to change.

To exit a meeting, tap on the 'End Meeting' on the bottom-right corner. Select 'Leave Meeting' in the window that appears, which will allow you to exit.

The meeting will continue until everyone leaves individually or until the host presses 'End Meeting for All.' If you are using a mobile device, tap on 'Leave' denoted in the red in the top-right corner of the screen.

ADDITIONAL SPECIFIC TOOLS YOU WILL NEED TO USE THE VIDEOCONFERENCING FEATURES

- A laptop, mobile, smartphone, or tablet computer.

- Speakers, a microphone, and a camera mounted or connected to your monitor or your mobile device.

- Network Desktop, Mac, Linux, and Mobile Computer Specifications

YOU'LL BENEFIT FROM HAVING

A set of built-in microphone headphones, which can be attached to your computer or mobile device. Those may be headphones (hand buds) in-ear or headphones over the hand.

The microphone may be inserted into the wire or placed on a boom. Capable of wired or wireless headphones.

It is suggested using a pair of headphones with a microphone attached, as they will give you the ability to:

- Hear clearly

- Speak clearly

- Less background noise

Such types of headphones have a microphone.

If you don't have a set of microphones included, you can use a pair of headphones without an integrated microphone, and use the microphone built into your computer or mobile device.

You may use the speakers and microphones built into your computer or mobile device when you don't have headphones or a microphone.

Enable the Zoom app by pressing on the "Zoom conferences Application" button below: "Install the Zoom app".

ON PC

Notice where the file is being stored when you press the Download button.

This is renamed ZoomInstaller.exe, which usually saves to the folder of your Downloads.

Double-click on the installation file, until you open it.

Press Run in a pop-up window labeled "Open File."

ON MAC DEVICES

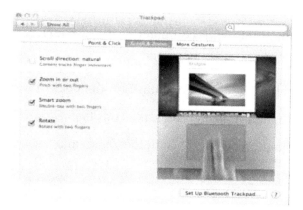

On Mac, the installation procedure is slightly more complex than on Windows because it involves changing some settings. You need to go to "System Preferences" (which can be called up by the apple symbol in the top left corner) and click on "Security and Privacy". From here you have to click on the padlock symbol at the bottom left to enable the changes. Finally, select the option "App Store and developers identified" under "Allow apps downloaded from:". Once this is done we can proceed to download Zoom from the official page. The file downloaded for macOS is "Zoom.pkg" on which you just need a double click to start the installation procedure that in a few steps will allow us to have Zoom on our Mac

You can copy the installer package, Zoom/Installer.pkg, into your Downloads tab.

Go to the Downloads tab in the Mac, and then double-click the installation file. Select start to operate the installation software, in the pop-up tab.

CREATING AN ACCOUNT

You can continue by adding your email address or heading to http:/Zoom.us/ and signing up with a free account. Tap the Zoom email to activate. Fill out your Email and password in this section When you have an email linked with Zoom, click https:/Zoom.us/download the Zoom software here.

SIGN IN TO ZOOM

Go to Zoom sign-in page with the link "Zoom.us/signin".
It will ask you about your email address and your password for Zoom. Fill in the tabs and click on "Sign In".
You can stay signed in longer on your Zoom account by clicking on "Stay Signed In" on the page.

IPAD

Do you have an iPhone or an iPad? Well, Zoom also exists as an app for iOS/iPadOS: let's see how to install it. First, open the App Store, tap on the white stylized "A" on a blue background, press the Search button (bottom right), type "Zoom" in the search bar at the top, and, in the screen that opens, tap on ZOOM Cloud Meetings (the blue icon on which the camera is drawn).

Now, tap the Get button located at the ZOOM Cloud Meetings app and, if necessary, confirm the download via Face ID, Touch ID, or your Apple account password.

CHAPTER 3:

How To Use Zoom With Mobile Phones And An iPad

One of the market leaders at the marketing space, Zoom, is well known around the world because of its meeting room alternatives. If you're searching for outstanding usability video, and reliability, you cannot go wrong. Just before their Initial Public Offering started in April 2019, Zoom declared a ton of upgrades such as updated Zoom Rooms upgrades to Zoom Meetings. Here is everything you want to learn more about the cloud calling approach delivered through Zoom.

THE CHARACTERISTICS OF ZOOM PHONE

Zoom Phone is a simple cloud-calling solution constructed for users that wish to install calls. You would turn into Zoom if you do not require the meetings; you can start a VoIP phone that is fast using the tools you already know and enjoy. Zoom turns complete with messaging, voice, messaging, and video at precisely the same solution.

THE BENEFITS OF ZOOM PHONE

Perhaps Zoom Phone's biggest benefit is its ease of use. The application is intended to be as available as the remainder of the Zoom encounter, and therefore you don't have to download some applications that were intricate to utilize it. From video to voice calls, you can transition to using Zoom Phone.

Rewards include:

The simplicity of use for everybody: After you click in your Zoom customer, your Telephone function will just appear alongside your Chat and Assembly choices. Click on your telephone, enter the contact number or an individual's name, and you are all set to go. It is simple.

Connect to outside platforms: you can join your SIP alternative to outside programs from Five9 and Twilio too. In this manner, it is easier to handle your phone routing choices through a number of the world's favorite cloud phoning providers

BYOC: Zoom is dedicated to innovating as promptly as possible to their clients so they can deliver performance that suits the whole Zoom expertise. The Bring Your Carrier or BYOC alternative ensures You Could access all of the Benefits of Zoom Phone via your existing PSTN trunks

Centralized Communication Management: Zoom Telephone matches seamlessly into any consumer's digital transformation approach. The system enables companies and business leaders to manage and supply users publicly, track company interactions, and much more in an easy admin gateway

TARGET MARKET & REGIONAL AVAILABILITY

Zoom Phone is a great solution for any business that needs and adores the Zoom expertise the freedom calls, as well as meetings. The Telephone system enables workers to socialize on a program they are knowledgeable about. Australian beta support and the UK for Zoom Phone became accessible per petition on the 19th of May. Zoom will roll out the service to markets in the foreseeable future.

ZOOM DIFFERS ON YOUR PHONE, SO HERE IS THE WAY TO USE IT

Not everything works on the cellphone or the iPad as it does on your laptop. Different devices have different capacities, as Zoom describes on its site in addition to its own Google Play and Apple App shops. Although the company does not say it specifically, the Zoom on your phone or tablet computer isn't quite as powerful as the version for

Mac or Windows. Just examine screen sharing or the chat attributes on cellular. But that does not mean the program does not work for certain scenarios.

VIEW MANNERS

Anecdotally, it appears Zoom's mobile program is not too popular for work meetings because many men and women want the entire display to see graphs, files, and all of your colleagues also from the assembly. If your requirements are more productivity-focused, stick with that notebook for Zoom. The screen options that are limited to others are shown. On the Zoom cellphone, you may have four faces to display at one time correctly.

But in your notebook, it is similar to credits opening. Gallery perspective lets up to 25 participants on a display since the Zoom website explains.

CHATTING

Zoom Background to Get A Smoother Experience

The Zoom conversation is its own thing. You can message everybody on a telephone or only message a player. It is refreshingly retro in its simplicity. The dialog slots on the side of this display or whether you are in full-screen mode becomes a floating window. However, when you begin using the conversation on cellular, it isn't quite as simple to use, or perhaps find.

Clicking on the "More" button at the bottom of the program brings a conversation alternative that then brings up a window which takes over the whole telephone and... it is just messy. With the Zoom background experience, stick for side effects.

Screen sharing

You can present your display by telephone, but it is not as easy as a procedure as on desktop. If you are introducing a slideshow or active display, your notebook will be simpler to share. It may get bizarre sharing your telephone display.

MULTITASKING

Let us be real here: You are not committed to just your Zoom call. If you are not introducing or leading a meeting, it is simple enough to look as if you are paying attention when doing anything else in your notebook. In your telephone, however, it is a little more of a hassle to browse to your email inbox.

VIDEO

One of my co-workers uses the Zoom program on his Mobile Phone, especially because of its video purpose -- he utilizes a rack so that the phone is an outside camera beside his PC. Then there are the seconds you might want to maneuver around through a Zoom telephone number. You are less likely nowadays to be commuting in the car (although you might be on the road to the supermarket), but only because you are trapped in your home does not mean that you want to be tethered to a notebook or portion of the home designated as "the office." The cellular program provides you with some freedom to move around, do some home chores, or look after the kids.

BACKGROUNDS

You can alter your background on the iOS and variations, thank goodness. It is not for Android consumers, sorry! However, so long as you've got an iPhone newer or 8, you are set for cellular. Your desktop game can go large. In case you've got a laptop. For computers, it can't probably be handled by the operating system. This may help you keep it professional.

ZOOM CALLS FOR MICROSOFT

What's not to enjoy about Zoom Phone? Is there a drawback to moving from a UC platform such as Microsoft Skype for Business? Here are some important things to think about:

Characteristic Parity: Zoom is devoting substantial resources to the item. At precisely the same time, some marketplace views are that mobile cloud system offerings are still not 'feature complete' compared to other UCaaS platforms. But this attribute completeness view is used to explain Microsoft teams. For a long time, it was utilized in reality to explain Microsoft Skype for business. In Microsoft instances, the traditional wisdom of the marketplace has not ceased the Redmond juggernaut from winning the UC market share. Why should it be any different with Zoom Phone?

Shadow IT Legacy: Oftentimes, the rapid adoption of Zoom Video Conferencing happened with no first sponsorship of IT. While this type of transformation may happen quite fluidly with automation, on-prem, or cloud PBX may be different animals. Just as Zoom has charmed the ending --consumer, in some instances they are playing catch up on the telephone side with more conventional enterprise IT departments.

UC and UCaaS Incumbent Speed Bumps: Vendors such as 8×8 and RingCentral now occupy thoughts share in the pristine UCaaS planet, and UC sellers Microsoft, Cisco, and Avaya will be the conventional on-premises incumbents.

These elderly UC/UCaaS companies introduced dread, doubt, and uncertainty on functioning through budgeting, system depreciation, migration, and dependability. Paradoxically, many people think that the Zoom phone is more enterprise-ready compared to several standard players.

There remain speed lumps in the test procedure in front of IT that can embrace a Zoom Cloud PBX move.

Tracking & Troubleshooting Depth: The box Zoom management portal makes it possible for businesses to manage and supply users, track company interactions, and exhibit service performance metrics. But some innovative IT teams still feel as they demand more advanced monitoring thickness, higher flexibility, the capability to concurrently track and troubleshoot multiple UC platforms, also, above all, actionable insights that guide IT exactly on how and where to fix issues. As with other programs such as Microsoft or Cisco, there are.

Zoom Success: Zoom's excellent achievement in the video conferencing area, coupled with siloed casual pilots of Zoom Phone during many ventures, might be contributing to a general Cloud PBX slow-down. The upside for Zoom is that associations pause to appraise all cloud telephone choices (like Zoom Phone) in much more detail. The possible drawback is a more comprehensive analysis could let it slow down a complete Zoom Phone program should they determine that crucial requirements are missing.

ZOOM CLOUD PBX ON THE UPSWING

The UCaaS marketplace might reach a value of greater than $79 Billion by 2024 up from approximately $8 billion based on some 2019 report from Transparency Market Research. In parallel, according to its standing as a major video conferencing platform, the head talk of Zoom, premature, and buzz transformation victories for Zoom Phone are powerful. There is a lengthy list of reasons to consider piloting Zoom Phone strongly:

Flexible deployment versions: Zoom Phone may be deployed in several geographical areas due to the platform's capacity to leverage existing suppliers or utilize third-party SIP trunking and calling programs.

BYOC (Bring Your Carrier): Nearly a mirror image of Microsoft's Direct Routing capacity, Zoom alternative helps to ensure you could access all of the benefits of Zoom Phone via your existing PSTN trunks. This special capacity gives organizations each the advantages and characteristics of Zoom Phone while maintaining existing service supplier contracts, telephone numbers, and calling speeds using their favorite carrier of the document and when desired, an incumbent PBX.

Communications endpoint options: Zoom Phone has allowed businesses the ability to select among desktop, IP, telephones, and headsets. Much more importantly, the Zoom cloud mobile system supports off-the-shelf components (without needing any kind of a complex certification program as with other sellers). This gives flexibility related to IT to proprietary heritage systems.

Frequently Asked Questions: That is not necessarily a sign of Zoom's capacity to provide, but we believe the character of the Zoom Phone FAQs (e.g., e911, local number portability, etc.) are indicative of the maturity of this platform.

Zoom + Slack: The two sellers lately introduced a new integration that will let users begin Zoom Phone calls inside Slack. Connection and the Slack fame with Zoom aid to enlarge the calling sway of Zoom.

Ecosystem: To encourage Zoom Phone, Zoom hauled partners that have cloud mobile system experience and has brought a number of the conferencing partnerships that were based. Additionally, in comparison to some of the UCaaS opponents, Zoom has become flexible, nimble, and quick to market with their APIs and mobile/desktop software development kits (SDKs). This permits programmers to create software and applications to improve the end-user and IT encounter.

ZOOM PHONE ENHANCEMENTS MAKE IT A POWERFUL ALL-IN-ONE GLOBAL OPTION

It is one of these communications platforms which rightfully receive a whole lot of press thanks.

Zoom has gained a reputation as being among the very first communications alternatives available on the marketplace, which had a laser focus on giving a high definition experience for both video and audio conferencing. This week, the business has announced plans to fortify further its support attributes regarding messaging, chat, and phoning.

The applications of Zoom are a substantial player in the internet conferencing stadium, and the firm has a history of shoring up any difficulties and fast releasing new attributes.

With this latest upgrade, Zoom Chat, Zoom Meetings and Webinars, and Zoom Phone have received updates that are certain to streamline procedures and fortify cooperation within organizations.

ZOOM PHONE HAS POWERFUL COLLABORATIVE MESSAGING

Firms like Zoom know that organizations need to ensure that workers can communicate with their teams to boost their communications that are unified profiles. UCaaS technology, which permits chat is very popular since the discussion is fast and simple to use without bothering workflows. Now, with this latest upgrade to Zoom Chat, users will have the ability to respond or add responses to prerequisite messages rapidly. User experience enhances by enabling a line of text or icons.

This type of attribute makes communications faster, and besides, it makes it simple for users to talk via their cellular devices or in their workplace. Additionally, @all mentions enable users to send a virtual "burst" through the cloud system to members of a group. This will work, so this is helpful for cooperation in addition to product or project management. A broadcast-quality that permits users to broadcast messages enhances this. Other societal functionalities such as @mentions and _station can also be available so that consumers may consult with a co-worker by title or reach out from particular channels easily. The contact profile attribute has been updated. When messaging a staff member, mousing over their title will disclose their division, their job name, as well as place. This attribute is handled and set up by admins through SAML mapping. However, it provides a superb amount of identification for groups, and every team member could manually update their data.

CONFERENCING AND WEBINAR TOOL UPGRADES

Video conferencing and audio are a few of the crucial attributes; therefore, it should not be surprising that the corporation would wish to augment the attributes offered in Zoom Meetings. To the program, display sharing can be restricted with the upgrade. This is very helpful for those presenters that wish to reveal a slideshow or a deck with no mistaking the attendees. This is suitable for maintaining data. Zoom has enhanced the waiting space solution's performance. For a meeting, participants may wait patiently in Zoom Rooms or could be routed there when information is being shared. The new functionality enables messages to be sent by hosts. All these are messages; therefore, it will not be redirected into the procedures of the assembly that is a video.

The waiting room encounter is being improved, so there's support for waiting rooms as a player in addition to a server. Into training or the seminar, attendees can bring their interpreters for organizations. This may cause some notions to be lost in translation. But with the newest simultaneous interpretation attribute, Zoom video calling provides the initial sound together with the translation, which enables listeners to pick up on tonal cues throughout the conference/webinar. Extra noise in the presenter's area could be picked up, although Zoom is well known for its HD quality. Zoom is implementing an innovative sound suppression feature that may cancel out background sound, to help enhance the expertise.

Zoom gives a phone recording functionality that's offered to paid subscribers -- there is a function. However, for the sake of confidentiality, alternatives like those need to have explicit approval practices after recording. A brand-new attribute for Zoom meetings enables administrators to customize the permission pop-up -- provided that they've Zoom 4.6.0 or afterward. Ultimately, for Zoom Chat and Zoom Meetings, users will have the ability to share and upload documents. The box is a business-grade storage system that also presents exceptional collaboration and workflow performance, so simple integration with Zoom gifts a fantastic way to share documents while at a meeting or a conversation safely. To take advantage of your seminar, take a look at our guide about the best way best to make a webinar train or market solutions.

AUDIO COMMUNICATION ENHANCEMENTS FOR ZOOM PHONE

We adore Zoom Voice for communications. Zoom, at its heart, is a communications solution that offers telephony for your staff cooperation processes and to the customer outreach of your team. To fortify this baseline communications performance, the Zoom Phone support was updated to give accessibility in Ireland, New Zealand, and Puerto Rico, also beta testing was introduced to Austrian, Belgian, French, Dutch, Danish, Italian, German, Portuguese, Spanish, Swedish, and Korean markets.

Additionally, for those searching with other possibilities, Zoom has community peering with Genesys cloud contact center alternatives. This will allow for the phone Zoom permits to dial-up from anywhere, no matter if they are employing an iPhone, an Android, or whenever they are stuck making telephone calls. Voice call quality enhancements and cellular programs mean a reliable and constant platform for communications. Is it implementing a system setup of a Zoom Phone program? If that's the case, Zoom IP desk phone templates, which could differ throughout a company with phone numbers and ports, can be defined by administrators. This may simplify the practice of utilizing Zoom along with the PBX cloud mobile system considerably, or you're SIP.

THE ZOOM COMMUNICATION AND RECRUITING PLATFORM IS IMPROVING

All these features will enhance the Communications expertise for SMBs, and each is implemented thanks to the very user-friendly layout of Zoom. Added features like fresh program execution on the Zoom Marketplace support for Korean and domain developments illustrate the organization's devotion to maintaining the encounter aggressive and up-to-date for users.

CHAPTER 4:

How To Protect Your Account

ZOOM SECURITY ISSUES

Z oom is the unquestioned leader in the market when it comes to digital conferencing software. The blend of in-depth functionality, elegant design, and accessible pricing structure allows it a worthy addition to the application framework of every company. Only note to take maximum advantage of all of the services that are provided by Zoom. If you do, you will enjoy all the benefits Zoom has to bring. The program you choose will rely on the team's scale, how much you expect to utilize Zoom, the intent to use the method, and the existing budget.

There were some security issues when the Zoom application was launched. With increased demand, the Zoom organization takes into account of its security issues and updates. The organization has created several movements to counter security issues and reassure users that security and privacy are essential. That involves necessary items like deleting the meeting identifier from the call's title bar. The organization has announced multiple changes to the program to improve protection credentials. Before you continue utilizing the platform for your business and other purposes, you must understand the privacy and security issues of the platform.

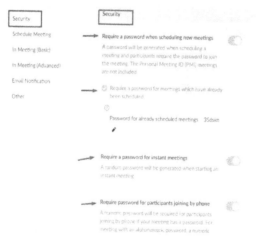

The platform claims to utilize the end-to-end concept of encryption, and that means that it should not have access to video and audio communications. However, the reverse is the case, and the platform can access, host a video meeting, interaction, and serve several other purposes at any given time and location. It is a flaw that can jeopardize important information distributed through the platform.

There have been lots of reports about data privacy issues associated with the platform. There are several tasks you can perform on the service, which includes a record of meetings, documents, and generated texts while the meeting was going on. You should also know that organizations with paid accounts have lots of control over their workers. They can join any meeting hosted by any worker and also keep track of their data without permission or knowledge.

Safety tips are needed to prevent unnecessary and unwarranted access to your Zoom meeting.

WAITING ROOM SAFETY TIPS

The urgent need for an online video conferencing tool that works during this era of COVID-19 when people have started working from home has led to the rise in the number of people using the Zoom app daily. That said, the increase in the number of users has often led to a breach of privacies and securities- a menace Zoom is working all day to solve. To avoid an undue breach of your privacy, it is only pertinent you adopt safety tips that can guide you towards having a hitch-free session on Zoom. One of the ways to curb the issue of Zoom bombing is the Zoom waiting room. The Zoom waiting room allows organizers to access participants before entering meetings. This is necessary to ensure uninvited guests are disallowed from entering the meeting.

MEETING ID

Another effective way to foster security is through the use of random meeting IDs for every session. This is to disallow uninvited users from gaining access since you are won't use the same meeting ID for your next meeting. Try to avoid sharing the meeting ID on public media to prevent gate crashing.

MEETING PASSWORD

Try to enable the "request password for every session" on your Zoom. Make the password harder to guess by increasing the length of the numeric character.

MANAGE ATTENDEES

The meeting organizer should ensure he's the only host of the meeting at a time. The host should have the ability to mute any participant and disable them if needs arise.

BE CAREFUL WHEN CLICKING ON ANY MEETING LINKS

Attackers, sometimes, generate links that look like Zoom links to have access to your computer when you click such a link. Be wary of the links you copied, click, and share.

Zoom has recently has issues regarding security and issues such as screenshotting, revealing participants as well as combined with undesirable visitors known as Zoom bombers. This is when users get access to meetings and try to interfere by displaying forbidden materials in the meeting.

In any case, the organization has made a few moves to counter these issues and console clients about the significance of security and protection. This incorporates basic things like expelling the gathering ID from the title bar of the call so that if clients share screenshots online the meeting isn't presented to future maltreatment.

WHAT ARE ZOOM BOMBERS?

The ascent in unmistakable quality of Zoom has prompted the administration to be mishandled by web trolls and individuals with an excessive amount of time to burn. A few people have been chasing down open and unreliable Zoom gatherings just as giving themselves access, from there on "besieging" others on the call with realistic recordings, erotic entertainment, and other unseemly acts.

There are different ways you can keep this from happening, for example, making sure about your calls, forestalling screen sharing, and, in any event, impairing video. The people behind Zoom are likewise setting up measures to make sure about your calls and to guard them.

DEFAULT SECURITY REFRESHES

On the off chance that you don't realize Zoom has been refreshed with various security changes to help support clients. One of these various security changes has been the need for a password as default for Zoom gatherings. This, along with the virtual sitting areas, ensures that just those people who have been welcome to the called meeting are permitted in. This is one of the steps that ensure calls are sheltered and secure for everybody.

ZOOM SECURITY INSTRUMENTS

Zoom has likewise made it simple to oversee and make sure about your gatherings when they are going on. There is a scope of security instruments you can access with a few tricks which involve the capacity to leave the gathering when it has begun to keep new individuals from going along with you can likewise evacuate late members on the assemble just as quieting members with a debilitating private visit as well. Once more, to get to the security instruments Zoom, you can continue by tapping on the security button showing up in the window when a call is passing across a member to interface with them to evacuate them from the call.

REVEALING DIFFERENT MEMBERS

Besides, it is conceivable to report members on the call who are not welcome or are causing issues. For the motivation behind removing them from the call, it is conceivable to send a report to the Zoom Trust and Safety group to deal with abuse of the framework. This will further assist in squaring them from the administration in the future just as meddling with different calls as well. To do this, click the security button on the gathering and afterward click the report.

CHAPTER 5:

How To Use Zoom For Meetings And Video Conferences

VIDEO SETTINGS

Now, we will tweak the video settings. Click on 'Video' located above 'Audio' in the left panel. The Video Settings box will look like this.

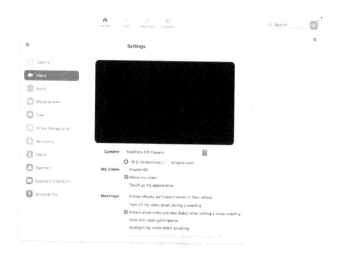

As soon as you click on 'Video', a box appears with a message saying, 'Zoom would like to access the camera.' Click on 'OK.' The black box in this picture will display what is seen by your front-facing camera. This is how the other participants will see you during the call. You can adjust your position and device to provide a clear view.

If you have other devices or webcams attached externally to your video interface, select the device from the dropdown menu beside 'Camera.' Leave the other settings as they are, and exit the box.

STOP VIDEO OPTION

Once your audio and video settings are in place, you are good to go. Close the setting page and click on the button "New Meeting" to start a meeting. If you need the call to be just audio, you can select the 'Stop Video' option on the bottom-left corner of the window, as you access to the meeting.

INVITE NEW PARTICIPANTS

The next step will involve inviting participants to the call. Select the 'Participants' option on the bottom panel of the window, and then click on "Invite".

You will see a window that looks like this.

You can either invite people from your contact list or via email. The easiest way is to click on 'Copy URL' and send the generated meeting URL with the people you wish to invite. Exit the box. Once you send this URL to the preferred participants, they can easily access the meeting by pasting this URL in their browser. You can also text or send the meeting password to your participants to join the discussion. We will elaborate further on this later in this section.

MANAGE PARTICIPANTS

We will now manage the participants that have permission to access the meeting. Click on 'Participants' on the bottom panel of the main window.

You will see a popup that will display all the participants that have entered the meeting. It will look like this.

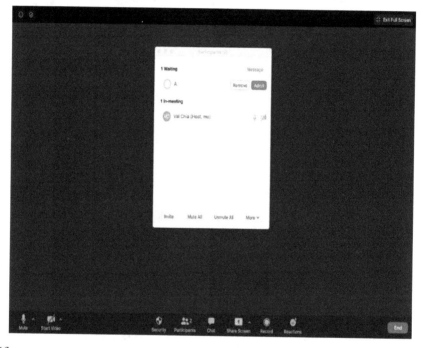

If you move your mouse over the participants' names, you can mute a particular participant or mute all of them by selecting 'Mute All' at the bottom. This functionality is extremely useful when a single person is in need to speak or is instructing everyone.

HOW TO PREPARE YOURSELF TO WORK WITH VIDEO CONFERENCES AND ONLINE MEETING

SKIP THE MUNDANE DETAILS

They have a radius. No, seriously... Consider it like this: When the essential points are those that strike at home? They are in the middle of your circle. You are veering off-center ever, as you get into more detail about each stage in your outline. As you venture farther from the middle, you are raising your radius. Now that you know what we mean by the term "radius," then you may use this value to quantify just how mundane the details on your dialog are. You begin having a big radius; if you get started branching into subtopics of subtopics within an obscure part of your outline, your audience will be lost.

The radius not merely steps how mundane your demonstration is; it also measures how far off you are pushing your crowd from you. Do not send them. Point-blank selection takes for the majority of your demonstration.

Do not allow over just a few inches to grow. Keep it easy, and flowing with the thoughts, if you have to enter detail. When there's a great deal of detail, think about passing it out at a thorough handout they could read afterward and only going through the large points of this handout in person. Besides all this discussion of geometry, there is something else that you can do.

USE SLIDES

Boredom is a transmissible disease. If you are not careful, you'll send your training into something known as the FarmVille Zone: the time at a webinar when they will open up FarmVille and begin milking their small digital cows. Consider it that a webinar has come to be so stiff that the viewers would click farm critters than to what the presenter must say, listen. Is everything on these slides crucial to the demonstration? Is it something that the audience must understand to be able to follow along? You will likely come across fifteen, or even a slide, while preserving the integrity, which you can cut out. Use slides to push a few factors.

DETACH YOURSELF

If you are organizing a demonstration, your objectivity goes out the window. You've worked hard on obtaining this demonstration, and we are asking you to whip out a machete onto it. That is the reason it's so vital to have somebody else take a look at the demonstration and provide you with an honest review of what should or shouldn't be contained inside. In reality, you ought to have three or more folks look at it at a session that is brainstorming/chopping, which can make the assembly more intriguing. In this manner, you obtain an objective perspective. Everything you can do with their information is all up to you, but you must take all your small webinar "commission" states into significant consideration.

ENGAGED AUDIENCE SEGUE FROM ONE STAGE TO ANOTHER

Comedians, the best news anchors, and also the orators have made use of this segue. This tool makes presentations because it highlights things. Do not create your presentations move without easing the subject that is new in. You've all seen examples of the tool around this bit from the paragraphs. See that's taken good care of and attempt to add elements to your presentation!

USE ZOOM

Zoom Video Webinar is immersive. Not only can users take part in text Q/A and view your demonstration, but they could also understand the panel of presenters. Take good care of the way you look at the video! You may remove lots of those problems that plague conventional meeting solutions along with hosting presentations!

CHAPTER 6:

Zoom Features You Need To Know About

Z oom is a modern communication with an easy to use and reliable cloud platform for video and audio conferencing, collaboration, messaging, and webinars. It has many features and spans across various industries.

THE MAIN FEATURES OF ZOOM INCLUDE:

Zoom has many features that make the app desirable and well enough to compete with other video conferencing tools. These features range from user's ability to share files; share screens while working and record audio and video during meetings. With the increasing demands for Zoom, developers have up their games to ensure users' satisfaction comes first while maintaining the product's long-standing integrity. The following features are common in Zoom meetings:

GROUP VIDEO CONFERENCES AND WEBINARS

Zoom can host up to 500 participants (with the great meeting add-on). The free plan allows you to host video conferences up to 40 minutes and up to 100 participants. You can expand it to allow 10,000 viewers via Zoom webinars.

CALENDAR INTEGRATION

To make sure you don't miss your video conference or meeting, Zoom offers a reminder you can schedule a reminder between 5, 10, or 15 minutes before your session.

WAITING ROOM

All participants can't connect or join at the same time. There will always be participants that will join early and others late. Hence the critical reason for setting up a "waiting room." To be sure of who comes into a meeting, Zoom has featured a waiting room that enables participants to be clear fully. This feature makes sure you are aware of who comes into your meeting or conference by enabling the Waiting Room feature and admitting your participants for better security. Admit one participant or everyone at once, and even send a message to those waiting. As the meeting or conference host, you can admit attendees one by one or hold all attendees in the lounge and admit all of them directly. You can send all participants or only guests to the room when they join your meeting. Participants will see the subsequent display screen when joining the meeting or conference when the waiting room feature enabled: To enable this feature, after selecting "Program" on the home page of the app, select "Advanced options". Then you can then check the "Activate the waiting room" box and "Open access to the meeting room before the moderator arrives." In this way, if you are the organizer of the meeting, your delay will probably be better digested by your collaborators.

CLOSED CAPTIONING

Capture all spoken words with closed captioning for the deaf and hard of hearing. Zoom integrates with third-party captioning providers via our REST Closed Captioning API for the deaf and hard of hearing.

TOUCH-UP MY APPEARANCE FEATURE

When enabled, Touch-up My Appearance gives a soft focus for your whole screen that will make you look professional and ready.

The containment places pressure on our bodies, and you can notice on the screen. If the absence of exposure to a natural ray of light is felt on your skin, Zoom has a feature that will nearly imperceptibly enhance your appearance. This feature can be enabled by merely going to Settings, then to video, and click on the Touch-up my appearance button.

ACTIVATE HD MODE FOR BETTER IMAGE QUALITY

To maintain your internet connection, HD mode is disabled by default on Zoom. to reactivate it, go to the "Video" tab in "Settings" and check the "Activate HD video" field. Use it in the evening, when those who are telecommuting do no longer need the network.

AUTOMATIC TRANSCRIPTIONS

Make your understanding easier with automatic transcriptions. Transcripts are automatically generated and synchronized to facilitate discovering and viewing meeting or conference recordings.

KEYBOARD SHORTCUTS TO MOVE BETWEEN THESE FEATURES

Zoom enables keyboard shortcuts to activate one of its features during a video conference quickly.

To access their list, go to the "Keyboard shortcuts" tab in "Settings." Keyboard keys are registered by default. For a better grip, do not hesitate to change them yourself by clicking on one of the combinations in the "Shortcut" column.

KEYBOARD ACCESSIBILITY

Quickly complete all of your essential workflows using a keyboard. Zoom enables Keyboard Shortcuts for convenient navigation of Zoom features.

SCREEN READER SUPPORT

Use Zoom without a screen. We follow the latest accessibility requirements to make sure of the full accessibility of the product to the newest display screen readers.

ZOOM ROOM CONTROLLER

To have access to the Zoom control board, your device must be on either of the following OS; apple iPad running on iOS version 8.0 and above; android tablet running OS 4.0 and above, windows tablet running version 10.0.14393 or later, Crestron Mercury.

You need to download the Zoom Room controller from the Zoom download page. The following features are accessible with the Zoom Room controller:

Meet now

- Schedule meeting now with a selected number of participants.

- Contact list display for participants.

- Meeting list

- Display today's meetings list of participants

- Get upcoming meeting alerts.

- Joining a meeting

- Join a meeting using the meeting ID.

Presentation

- Start your meeting while still sharing the screen.

- Set screen sharing duration

Phone

- Switching from a phone Zoom call to a video session.

- Show call history.

- Device settings

- Select microphone

- Select speakers

- Web settings

- Private meeting

- Hide meeting ID.

ZOOM VISITOR CONTROL

The first thing you must ensure is that you have total control of your screen during meetings. You must deploy strategies to keep sanity in the meeting room. This is where visitor control comes in. You do not want a case of Zoom bombing where unwanted visitors are gate crashing your meeting and sharing un-savory contents. You can control the visitor's presence before meeting and even after meeting using your **host control bar**. To prevent unnecessary sharing of contents by visitors, make use of the host control bar. Tap the arrow beside the share screen menu to take you to the advanced sharing option. Locate the "who can share screen and choose" the only host." As part of Zoom's effective management of visitors and participants. There are features you must take note of. Follow these steps below to manage visitors effectively:

● Authorize the meeting so that only the invited participants can log in with their email.

● Generate a random Zoom meeting ID for all meetings. This will prevent gate crashing.

● Remove recalcitrant participants

● Disable video access to your meeting.

● Disallow private chat.

● Use the waiting room.

ZOOM VIRTUAL BACKGROUND

Instead of using the default Zoom background during Zoom meetings, you can make use of virtual backgrounds that can be downloaded online - or from your device pictures or videos. This works better with a green screen and a well-lighted room.

How to enable virtual background in Zoom

● Navigate to the Zoom web as an administrator and click on the Account settings icon.

● Enable the virtual background settings by navigating to the virtual background option.

● Log out of the Zoom desktop client and log in again for this feature to be appropriately activated.

How to enable virtual background for group members

- ○ Login to the Zoom web portal as an admin to edit users' group.
- ○ Select the group management icon.
- ○ Tap the name of the group and pick the settings icon.
- ○ Enable the virtual background settings on the meeting tab.

How to enable virtual background for personal use

- ○ Enter the Zoom Web Portal.
- ○ Access the "my meeting settings icon" if you are the administrator of the "meeting settings icon" if you're an ordinary member.
- ○ Enable the virtual background settings on the meeting tab.

To enable the virtual background for the Zoom room

- ○ Login to the Zoom Web Portal as an administrator.
- ○ Enter the Zoom room page and check-in account settings.
- ○ Turn on virtual background with a green screen on.
- ○ You can add more background pictures from your device's library if you want.

To enable a virtual background on windows

- ○ Log in to the Zoom desktop client.
- ○ Tap on your profile picture and choose settings.
- ○ Select virtual background
- ○ Toggle on" I have a green screen" if you already have it set up.
- ○ Select your desired virtual background image from the available ones. You can as well add them from your device's gallery.

BREAK OUT ROOMS

The Zoom break out rooms allows hosts to split Zoom sessions into more than one session.

It is only the account owner that can have access to this feature.

To enable Zoom break out rooms for all the members in your group:

o   Login into the Zoom web as an administrator that has the privilege to edit groups.

o   Access the navigation menu and click User Management and then Group Management.

o   Tap the name of the group, then choose the Settings tab.

o   Scroll down to the Breakout Room option on the Meeting tab to enable it

To enable Zoom break out room for your personal use.

o   Login to the Zoom portal.

o   Click Account Management from the navigation menu, and then click on Account Settings (provided that you're the administrator of the account) or Settings (if you are an account member).

o   Enable the Breakout Room option on the Meeting tab.

ZOOM WHITEBOARD

The Zoom whiteboard feature will give access to you (the host) and group members to share a virtual whiteboard with annotations. It works best on Zoom for Windows, Zoom for Mac, Linux, iPad, and Android.

Sharing a whiteboard on Windows:

- Tap the share screen icon in the toolbar.
- Select whiteboard
- Choose share.
- The annotations tools will be displayed. You can show and hide them from the whiteboard option
- Create and switch between pages by using the page control icon located at the bottom right corner of your whiteboard.
- Stop share when you are done.

Sharing whiteboard on Android

- Navigate to the meeting control and click on share.
- Choose the share whiteboard menu.
- Tap the icon that looks like a pen at the extreme left of the screen. This will open the annotation tools for writing and editing.
- Click on the *pin* icon again when you are done to close annotation.
- Stop share.

Sharing whiteboard on iOS: whiteboard only works on iPad for now, and not on iPhone.

- Click on share content available in the meeting control menu.
- Select whiteboard.
- The annotation tools will come up where you can edit and write texts.
- Tap "stop share" to stop sharing a whiteboard.

ZOOM RECORD MEETING

Tapping the record button at the bottom of your screen can enable you to record a meeting in Zoom. Recording meeting in Zoom is good, particularly if there is a particular colleague that should be in the meeting but was absent for one reason or another. The individual can always listen to the recording later to understand what has been discussed during the meeting. The organizer of the meeting must give access before you can record the meeting on Zoom.

Whether you want to keep a memory of your digital meetings or are simply too lazy to take notes during your work meeting, this feature could be useful for you. A recording is incredibly possible on Zoom and has a select tab in "Settings" with lots of advanced options.

Zoom recording on PC

- Tap the recording button at the bottom of your screen to start recording.
- Tap stop to end recording. The file will be stored as an MP4 on your computer.

Zoom recording on Android and iOS:

The same procedure is followed to record in both Android and iPhone devices. You must be on the Pro plan before you have access to records. Also, the meeting planner must grant you access.

- Open your Zoom app on Android or iPhone to join am ongoing meeting.
- Click on the three dots at the extreme right corner of your screen.
- Select record to the cloud (if you are using iPhone) or record (for Android).
- You can stop recording when you are done.

ZOOM CHAT

The Zoom chat is a new addition from Zoom to allow business users to chat securely. The chats are stored in local drives or Zoom cloud. Zoom chats add to the complete Zoom package where users can access real-time messaging platforms and share business ideas. The Zoom chat is available on both the mobile version and the desktop version. There is a premium account and a free account. Channels on premium accounts can have up to 5000 members or more while the free chat is limited to 500 persons. The Zoom chats are end-to-end encrypted; you do not need to worry about the security of data.

ZOOM REMOTE CONTROL

The Zoom remote control allows participants to control each other's screens while granting access. You can request remote control from the organizer who is sharing his screen. When he grants access, users can have the liberty to control what is happening on their screen.

How to request remote control on windows and Mac

Tap the view option drop-down menu to select request remote control. After the host grant access, you can then start controlling his screen by tapping inside the screen share.

To stop remote control, tap the view option drop-down again and choose to give up the remote control.

ZOOM SHARE SCREEN

The Zoom share screen is a common feature on Zoom for PC, tablets, and mobile devices. This feature allows participants to share what's on their screen for easy access by the group members. Co-workers, while working from home, can receive instructions and teach one another using their Zoom share screen. With this feature, you can see what the other members are doing on their computer screen. Only that the *shared screen* can only be done by the host if the account is basic. For premiums accounts, the host and the attendees can both share their screens.

The hosts do not necessarily need to grant access before other members can share their screens.

How to share screen on Windows and Mac

- Locate the share screen icon in the meeting control
- Choose the screen you want to share. You can even share Microsoft documents screen when opened.
- Tap the share icon to start sharing.

- The share screen will take up all your screen. You can exit the full-screen mode by clicking on the exit full-screen icon.
- While sharing your screen, you can access the following menus;
- Mute or unmute your microphone.
- Start or stop your video.
- If you are the host, you can view or manage the participants.
- Begin a new screen sharing.
- Pause your screen sharing mode
- Invite other participants to join your current meeting.
- Record the meeting to your computer storage or the Zoom Cloud.
- End the meeting at any time you want.
- Turn on the dual monitor option to be able to see both the participants and the screen you're sharing at the same time.

How to share your screen on Android devices:

sharing screen on Android requires Android 5.0 and later.

Sharing contents and files

- In the meeting Control, click on the share icon.
- A prompt will come up asking you which content you want to share. Choose the content you want to share.
- You can share photos, documents, whiteboards, website address, etc.

Sharing screens.

- Click the share icon in the meeting control.

- A list of available sharing options will be displayed. Choose screen.

- Click on "start now" to start.

- You can choose to share anything from your phone's desktop while Zoom keeps running in the background.

- You can stop sharing by tapping on stop share at the bottom of your screen.

HOW TO SHARE YOUR SCREEN ON iOS:

Needs iOS 11 or higher. You can share photos, iCloud Drive, Dropbox, whiteboard, etc. You can disallow any of these features from your account settings under the *integration* menu.

To share content

Click on share content directly from the meeting control.

Select the category of content you want to share.

If it is a document, you want to share, select *the document*, and choose the document from your Google drive.

To share the screen: Select the *sharing* icon and choose the *share screen*.

ZOOM KEYBOARD SHORTCUTS AND THEIR FUNCTIONS

You can explore Zoom settings on your Windows and Mac without necessarily using your mouse - just your keyboard. The shortcuts make accessibility easier for you.

Keyboard shortcuts for Mac users

The following are keyboard shortcuts for Mac users of Zoom:

Command(⌘)+J: To Join ongoing Meeting.

Command(⌘)+Control+V: To begin a Meeting.

Command(⌘)+J: To start Scheduling Meeting.

Command(⌘)+Control+S: To access the Screen Share via Direct Share.

Command(⌘)+Shift+A: To Mute or to unmute audio.

Command(⌘)+Shift+V: To begin or to stop the video.

Command(⌘)+Shift+N: Use to Switch camera

Command(⌘)+Shift+S: Use to Start or to stop screen share.

Command(⌘)+Shift+T: Use to Pause or to resume screen share.

Command(⌘)+Shift+R: To begin a local recording.

Command(⌘)+Shift+C: To begin cloud recording

Command(⌘)+Shift+P: To Pause or resume recording

Command(⌘)+Shift+W: Use to move to active speaker view or gallery view.

Control+P: To View the previous 25 participants in the gallery view.

Control+N: To View the next 25 participants in the gallery view

Command(⌘)+U: Use to Display/hide Participants panel.

Command(⌘)+Shift+H: To Show/hides In-Meeting Chat Panel.

Command(⌘)+I: Use to Open invite window

Option+Y: Raise hand/lower hand during the Zoom meeting.

Command(⌘)+Shift+F: Use to enter or to exit full screen.

Command(⌘)+Shift+M: Use to Switch to a minimal window.

Ctrl+Option+Command+H: To Show or to hide meeting controls

Ctrl+Shift+R: Have access to the remote control.

Ctrl+Shift+G: Withdraw remote control

Ctrl+\: Activate the "Always Show meeting controls" options in Settings.

Command(⌘)+W: To end or leave the meeting.

Command(⌘)+K: Switch to chatting mode with someone.

Command(⌘)+T: To take a quick Screenshot.

Command(⌘)+W: Use to Close any current window.

Command(⌘)+L: navigates between Portrait and Landscape View.

Ctrl+T: To switch between tabs.

Keyboard shortcuts for Windows

F6: Use to Navigate among Zoom popup windows.

Ctrl+Alt+Shift: Use during Zoom meeting to Move focus to Zoom's meeting controls

Alt+F1: Switch to active speaker view during a video meeting.

Alt+F2: Use to Switch to gallery video view in video meeting.

Alt+F4: Use to Close any current window.

Alt+V: Use to Start or to stop the video.

Alt+A: Mute/unmute audio

Alt+M: Use by a host to Mute/unmute Zoom audio for participants

Alt+S: Use to begin the share screen window and stop screen share

Alt+Shift+S: Enable users to Start or stop new screen share

Alt+T: Use to Pause or to resume screen share

Alt+R: Use to Start or to stop local recording.

Alt+C: Use to Start or to stop cloud recording.

Alt+P: Use to Pause or resume Zoom recording

Alt+N: Use to Switch camera

Alt+F: To Enter or exit full-screen mode.

Alt+H: To Display/hide the In-Meeting Chat panel.

Alt+U: Use to display or to hide any Participants panel

Alt+I: To Open any Invite window.

Alt+Y: To Raise or to lower your hand during meetings.

Alt+Shift+R: Access Remote Control

Alt+Shift+G: Withdraw Remote Control

Ctrl+2: Use to read active speaker name

Ctrl+Alt+Shift+H: Use to Show or to hide any floating meeting controls.

Alt+Shift+T: To take Screenshot on the Zoom screen.

Alt +L: To Switch between Portrait and Landscape View.

Ctrl+W: Use to close any current chat session.

Ctrl+Up: Back to previous chat

Ctrl+Down: Switch to the next chat

Ctrl+T: To switch to chatting mode with someone.

Ctrl+F: To Search any item.

Ctrl+Tab: Move to the next forward tab.

Ctrl+Shift+Tab: Use to move to the previous tab.

POLLS

You can go in and add a poll.

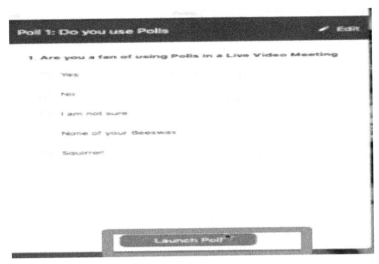

Enter the title for the poll, put in your question, set in the answers, and then you can post the poll and can save and share it with the group you plan sharing it.

If you're a little bit more organized, you can set up the poll in advance, actually, the first time I tried this as well, I did find it a little bit confusing and thought a lot of you will have the same confusion. If you schedule a new meeting, when setting up a new meeting in the Zoom, they tell you the polling features are right down at the bottom of this registration window when you're setting up all of the assets.

Still, if you take a look at this one, it's not there, there's no place to set up the poll when I scroll down to the bottom. But if I save the meeting, which means that you've got it scheduled then when you go down to the bottom of the screen.

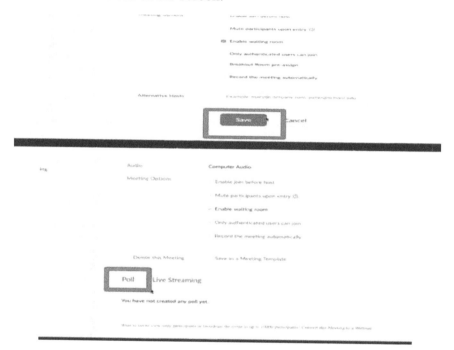

The polling feature appears, sand you can add by clicking, you might add, get the same dialog box that we were looking at, that will allow you to add a poll at this point. So that's how you can add a poll on the fly. Or you can add a poll in advance before the meeting starts.

CHAPTER 7:

Easy Tips For How To Solve Possible Technical Problems

U sers may encounter a couple of setbacks while using this app. Nevertheless, these glitches can be fixed in no time without requiring a high level of expertise and technical know-how

PROBLEMS ASSOCIATED WITH AUDIO-VISUAL

Just in case you joined a meeting and you can't hear anything, there's a likelihood you closed the first window that appeared. Ideally, you should select Join with computer audio, alternatively tap the spacebar on your computer or if using an android device, you can tap the audio button, if the audio is muted, you'll find the microphone sign crossed, you can simply tap this button to unmute it. Also for your camera/webcam, all you need to activate it is to tap the camera icon, if this doesn't work, you'll have to go to your camera settings and grant access to the app, for a computer, turn on the option of Allow apps to access your camera under your camera settings

In cases with multiple audio-visual devices, make sure the correct device is toggled on in the settings for proper communication. To do this, go to settings, click video or audio as the case may be, and select the appropriate device

PROBLEMS OF MISSING FEATURES

There could be an absence of some features when Zoom is being accessed via the web as opposed to the app. They've also been complaints of longer time being taken for web users to connect to an online meeting and some don't eventually connect at all. To solve this problem, just download the Zoom app from your play store if using an android device or from your apple store if using an iPhone, then you can enjoy all the features available to Zoom users

PROBLEMS WITH BACKGROUND NOISE/ECHO

Background noise/echoes are quite common especially when attendees don't mute microphones after joining the meeting, this way different activities occurring in their background filters in constituting a nuisance. It's important to note that this problem wouldn't exist if all users mute their microphone with just that of the host on, of course

Notwithstanding, the host can checkmate this at the entrance by disabling the microphones of all attendees, hence their microphones are muted by default, to do this, select the participant button, click more, and then choose the option of 'Deactivate participants at the entrance', there's also an option of 'Mute All' after tapping the Participant icon, this completely annuls background noise throughout the meeting

PROBLEMS RECEIVING THE ACTIVATION EMAIL

At times, it could take a while to receive activation emails, in some cases, just a few seconds, there's no hard and fast rule about it, it will eventually come. You can also check if the email wasn't sent to your spam folder

THE PROBLEM ASSOCIATED WITH A TIME LIMIT

Hosts should bear in mind that group meetings are permitted to last for only 40 minutes if you're on the free plan. Once the time elapses, all attendees have disconnected automatically, and the meeting brought to a sudden end

Another limitation is that you cannot record in the cloud, which means that sharing a recording with your team takes a little longer. Free users can record a meeting on their device, after which they can download the recording to Google Drive or another similar service, and then share it with others. It may or may not be a big deal for you, but it is something to keep in mind.

PROBLEMS WITH FREEZING /LAGGING DURING MEETINGS

A viable way of curtailing this is ensuring that you have good internet access, changing your location could just do the trick, make sure you also use a reliable service provider with a good internet speed {a range of at least 800kbps-1Mbps}

To ensure premium video quality, you should consider disabling the HD/Touch up my appearance option; this solves the problem of lagging

PROBLEMS WITH ZOOM CRASHING

If the app keeps closing/crashing abruptly, you can check Zoom service status to rule out the possibility of a locality issue, this can also be experienced when the server is undergoing servicing, it usually returns to normal after servicing is completed

If it's not a locality issue, you can switch from the app to the web version; this is more efficient in such cases as far as you have good internet access

It's important to ensure your audio-visuals are routed to the proper channel, audio to speakers and video to the webcam as the case may be, ensure this is done in the settings

PROBLEMS WITH ZOOM-BOMBING

Zoom bombing is the deliberate act of disrupting a meeting via the use of various tools like inappropriate videos, gestures, comments. It's become imperative to secure your meetings from ill-meaning individuals

TECHNICAL REQUIREMENTS TO SET UP ZOOM

Zoom in for professionals and as such requires devices that can meet some technical requirements to function properly. There are some operating systems supported by Zoom and you must make sure your device conforms to the requirements if you want to enjoy Zoom. Here, we will take a look at system requirements for both PCs and smartphones.

TECHNICAL REQUIREMENTS FOR PC, MAC, AND LINUX.

System requirements:

- *RAM requirement:* The operating system must have at least 4GB RAM.
- *Processor:* Core i3,i5,i7 or AMD equivalent system.
- *Supported browser:* Google Chrome, Safari, Mozilla Firefox.

A perfect internet connection, let's say a 3G/4G wired or wireless Inbuilt Camera in good working condition. Sometimes, a webcam can be fitted to the system for effectiveness.

Microphone and speakers: it might be a Bluetooth enabled or USB plug-in.

Operating system supported by Zoom: The following OS works better on Zoom - Windows 10, Windows 7, Windows 8 or 8.1, Window Vista with SP1, Windows XP with SP3, Oracle Linux 6.4 or upgraded version, Mint 17.1 or more, Fedora 21 or upgraded version, Ubuntu 12.04 or upgraded version, Red hat enterprise Linux 6.4 or more, Open SUSE 13.2 or more, Arch Linux, Mac OS X with MacOS 10.7 or more.

ZOOM TECHNICAL REQUIREMENTS FOR SMARTPHONES

- A cellular internet connection or Wi-Fi
- *Operating system:* iOS 8.0 or advanced, iPad OS 13 and above, Android 5.0 and above.
- *Processor:* 1Ghz single core or upgraded
- *Browsers*: Safari 5+ and chrome for iOS. Chrome for Android

CHAPTER 8:

Tips On How To Perform Best On Video

Zoom video conferencing can be a staple of modern communications, but the technology is still young enough for room for improvement. A video conference can be either the best thing on Earth or one of the most uncomfortable things you can imagine, depending on how you plan.

Zoom is the best video conferencing solution, but it's just one piece of the video conference experience. To make participants feel as if they meet face-to-face, the entire process needs to be seamless.

You'll need the right hardware and, maybe, a minor shift in the way you use your computer to make your interactions with others come alive. If you are using a tablet or cell phone, hardware options may not have as much versatility as desktop computers, but there are still things you can do to improve your experience. Let's look at the elements required for an excellent video gathering experience:

Online conferencing service Zoom provides more and such features, a number of the choices in menus. The hints and the tricks below will demonstrate how you can use the program to communicate with other people, understand, and operate. A few of the tips include ways in which you may link Zoom along with programs that are popular to automate your job.

PREPARE IN ADVANCE

Don't plug in at the last second only to find that your cat has bit the headset cable and the webcam needs a driver update to work. Access your video call app in advance, make sure everything is in order and, if there are any problems, you'll have time to resolve them relatively stress-free. If you use a laptop or smartphone, it's not a bad idea to make sure the battery is charged before the call starts.

COMMIT TO VIRTUAL WORKING

Virtual working, or working from home, isn't always as easy as it sounds. Sure, you have the flexibility and more time to get things done, but this might lead you into a spiral of procrastination.

For this to work, you need to commit. Now, this can be a challenge if you are new to it or are handling a large team. Handling and committing to a virtual working environment can be boiled down to two things: effective communication skills and enhanced productivity.

LET'S DIG DEEPER

As a boss, handling a team, particularly a virtual working team, can be one of the biggest challenges in the corporate world. The first thing you can do is encourage communication within the team. Make sure that your employees or colleagues are aware of the difference between a virtual working environment and an office job. Explain basic details, such as how you will communicate and what that looks like. An example can be holding trial video conferences to ensure effective communication in the future. Keep the video conferences concise. You can automatically enhance productivity by sticking to the point and explaining the project objectives in a precise manner. This will provide a clear explanation of your ideas and your employees or colleagues will not be caught up in frequent video conferences.

THE IMPORTANCE OF SCHEDULING

Scheduling is important even if you are working remotely. It might be more important if you tend to procrastinate or have a habit of delaying submissions and assignments. With proper scheduling, you can respect deadlines and get work on time. Treat your home as your workplace. When it comes to video conferences, schedule your calls beforehand, and inform the required participants about the meeting details. This should include the meeting ID or password (to enter the meeting), the topic of discussion, time, date, and duration of the meeting. Having prior knowledge of the meeting will ensure that your participants are thoroughly prepared and ready to actively engage in the conference. Even though it might seem unimportant, scheduling does help keep track of your operations, especially if you need to consult your team occasionally. Set reminders to alert you an hour before your meeting. You don't want to be late for a meeting that you host.

LET SOMEBODY ELSE SCHEDULE YOUR MEETINGS

Whoever manages your calendar is now able to program Zoom calls. To prepare, log into Zoom, open Assembly with Settings, and then search under others. You will see a plus sign. By checking their email addresses, insert your scheduling services by clicking Assign, and conclude. Once you include your scheduling programs, they log in to your attribute and need to log from Zoom. Using the Program tool from that point on, urges can create meetings too many others. Search to Advanced Options or Recruitment Options (depending on what type of Zoom you utilize) and follow the prompts to create a new assembly.

Prerequisites: The Principal Zoom account holder and everybody who receives scheduling rights must have Guru or Corp licenses. And such as webinars scheduler and account holder should have training permits.

AUTOMATICALLY SCHEDULE MEETINGS--AND LET PEOPLE KNOW ABOUT THEM

If you run a lot of meetings--for example, with customers and do not have an assistant, you may want to join Zoom, your scheduling program, along with your calendar. Whenever someone at a scheduling program books a scheduled appointment, Zapier can produce a new Zoom assembly and insert it. With all those programs you use below are a few Zaps to electricity this particular workflow. However, you can produce a Zap. You can add a to make this automation a stronger measure that shares the assembly details along with your group utilizing a program like Slack.

SET GOALS

Working from home, without physical assistance from your team, is tough. When you want to continue your business, you need to constantly consult and gel with your team. This is not entirely possible while working virtually. To be as effective as possible, you should set certain goals. Whether it relates to your year-end turnover or establishing communication within your team, a set of objectives will help you when you are working at a distance. Set goals, host a meeting, and communicate with your team over a video conference.

You may need to spend hours in the planning stages before you begin communicating with your employees.

Trim these goals into processes and tasks and assign them to relevant employees and departments.

Try to simplify the tasks as much as possible to maintain coordination among your team members. Keep a track of the tasks that you have assigned to your team members and stay connected virtually at all times.

Ensure clarity between your team members and conduct 'after-action' reviews once the deadlines are reached.

This practice might take up to 90 days for it to become routine, but once you do, you will close in on your target. Conduct trial sessions in between to keep the workflow stable.

Since there is a lack of constant communication and observation, ensuring productivity can be difficult.

Hold regular review meetings and convey your expectations about intermediate milestones despite a lack of face-to-face communication. The point is, you may need to learn to micro-manage to be a true leader with virtual meetings.

DO'S AND DON'TS

Assuming that you are on a formal call, there are certain dos and don'ts you should follow as an active participant.

CREATE AN APPROPRIATE SETUP

No one wants to look at a messy background when they are talking to you on a video call. Needless to say, a clean backdrop is mandatory to conduct any video call. After you clean your surroundings, start the video camera to test how your video call looks and to ensure that your backdrop is appropriate. Set the camera at an appropriate angle. Keep it at eye level to ensure that the other person can see you with ease. Ask family members or roommates to keep be quiet until the video conference ends or remove yourself from a noisy environment. Next, check the lighting. A backlight can be extremely uncomfortable and distracting for the other person. Stick to natural lighting or overhead lighting.

PAY ATTENTION AND STAY FOCUSED

Staying focused is necessary while on a video call because failing to do so can show a sincere lack of professionalism. Try not to send emails, look elsewhere, and don't check your phone. Many people have a habit of constantly looking at themselves on the screen. This shows a lack of attention to the other person and you could come across as self-centered. Even if you have to look away, communicate it to the person who is on the call with you and excuse yourself for a second. However, try not to do that in the first place. Since you are more visible on video conferences when compared to physical meetings, people will notice when you are distracted.

MUTE THE CALL WHEN THE OTHER PERSON IS SPEAKING

By muting a call, the other person can talk freely without being disturbed. This is particularly useful during group conference calls. Participants can become easily distracted due to unwanted noises in the background, which is why you should mute yourself when you are not speaking. Consider switching off your video too. If someone interrupts your call or if you need to tend to something, switching off your video is convenient. However, at times, the other person is unable to focus with switched-off video screens. Ask their permission first and act accordingly.

BE COURTEOUS

Needless to say, you should be courteous to the other callers and display basic manners while the call is ongoing. Introduce yourself and ask others for their names as well. Try to remember as many as you can and address them by their name whenever you can.

UNDERSTAND THE DIFFERENCE BETWEEN A VIDEO CALL AND AN EMAIL

Some people fail to understand the importance of a topic of discussion. At times, even if the topic could be successfully discussed over an e-mail or Slack, they decide to host a video conference, which is, in fact, completely unnecessary. Know the difference and stick to an email and you will not waste anyone's time. However, if the subject is intense and needs a verbal explanation for full comprehension, do not hesitate to schedule a video conference.

CHECK YOUR INTERNET CONNECTION AND SPEED BEFOREHAND

Before starting or participating in a video call, make sure that your internet setup is adequate.

Check the broadband connection and speed. Do a test video call with one of your close acquaintances to ensure the connection.

DO NOT INTERRUPT THE OTHER PERSON

Constant interruption is off-putting. Wait for your turn. You will know when it is your turn to speak

. If there is something urgent or important that needs to be spoken, give a signal, and then speak.

If your colleagues are planning to host these meetings constantly, work out a set of gestures for permission to speak or ask questions, like raising your hand.

You can also use the chat options available in most of the video conferencing services to ask a question or insert a comment without interrupting the flow of the speaker.

DO NOT MULTI-TASK

As mentioned, do not cause any distractions during the video call. Multitasking is the worst form of distraction. Eating, checking your phone, talking to someone else, etc., are major forms of distraction that should be avoided at all costs. Wait for the call to end or excuse yourself if it's extremely important.

DO NOT LOOK MESSY OR SLOPPY

Along with a clean backdrop, a clean appearance is also necessary during a video call, particularly during professional meetings. Dressing in your comfiest pajamas and sweatshirt is fine if you are attending a virtual family gathering, but with a professional call, you need to change to formal clothes, at least from the waist up if you are sitting through the entire call. Don't forget to neaten your hair. Dressing for your audience will leave an impression.

An Additional Tip: While conducting or participating in a video conference, agree on one language, and stick to it. This is specifically necessary if your video call involves people from all around the globe or for bilingual participants.

NOTICE WHO ATTENDED

Say you are using Zoom to maintain an event Lecture or even safety. You need to learn who snore. When the assembly is completed, you may find that info. The attendee list for many meetings resides from the Zoom Account Management > Reports department. Start looking for Usage Reports, and then click Assembly to obtain pick date range and the record type, and then create the report. Prerequisites: To create an attendee list, you have to be the 1) the sponsor of this assembly, 2) at a function with Utilization Reports empowered, or 3) an accounts owner or administrator. Besides, you require API Partner, a Guru, Business, or Education program.

COLLECT INFORMATION FROM ATTENDEES

You can collect info from meeting with attendees, alongside having an attendance sheet until they join the telephone. As an example, you may want to require that attendees provide their title, business affiliation, or business. To gather this information, you want to require registration, and an alternative located in the Zoom net app's My Meetings tab. You can establish a type before they could join the assembly that attendees need to fill out. For the enrollment form, Zoom offers fields, for example, title and business affiliation, that you add using checkboxes. Jump to the tab named Custom Questions to include disciplines or queries. If you are using an occasion to conduct such as a webinar, you may want to allow attendees to enroll utilizing a form in your site or an event management program.

It's possible to create this automation stronger by making certain is added to an email marketing instrument or a CRM, which means that you can follow up readily.

Prerequisites: To take attendee data in Zoom, the server has to have a Pro account. The assembly cannot be your Meeting ID.

DOCUMENT THE CALL AS A VIDEO

Zoom enables you to record your internet conferencing requirements—a feature for sharing the assembly for reviewing what has been stated. You have to decide whether to utilize the cloud or local alternative when you document. Local means you save yourself files, whether locally on your personal computer or in a different storage area that you supply. Using Cloud, that can be for paying members only, Zoom shops the video for you in its cloud storage (different account forms arrive with various levels of storage). One advantage of this cloud alternative is when it is ready, that individuals can stream the video through a web browser. It creates a large difference in the quality to maximize a few settings beforehand when creating a video phone. In which just the server looks on screen by way of instance, some calls may be broadcast-style. If that's the case, place Zoom to record video and the sound of this server. Forecasts may be in a meeting, in which case that you wish to document everyone's design. Make certain to research the configurations of Zoom for a couple of minutes.

Prerequisites: To Record videos, you will need Zoom on macOS, Windows, or even Linux. If you do not find the choice to record, assess your preferences from the web app (beneath My Meeting Settings) or have your accounts administrator empower it.

GIVE ATTENDEES A WAITING SPACE

Zoom enables the attendee's access to a phone without or with the host. Because they may have a couple of minutes to chit-chat until the meeting kicks off. A much better solution is to make a virtual living area, where attendees stay on hold till you let them all at precisely the same time or one by one. The way you empower a room is contingent upon the kind of account you have. However, it is possible to customize exactly what the attendees view while they wait for your entry when you set up one.

Conclusion

Zoom can be used in business meetings, distance learning, presentations, and other scenarios. For the Zoom app to function effectively, some rules are required of the user to adhere to. It is also advised for one to make use of an ample amount of lighting, and as well as good audio and cameras.

Zoom has various plans and each has its features which the said user can exploit, the basic plan of Zoom is pro bono but this basic account is limited to certain features of the Zoom app requiring the user to upgrade to other priced plan for better features.

Setting up and joining a Zoom meeting is one easy thing to do and there are many things one can do in a Zoom meeting such as recording of the meeting, sharing of the screen, etc.

Zoom can suit any workflow and can be used on a laptop or smartphone device. Such versatility is ideal for remote workers as any worker will function in a way that fits them better from wherever they may be. Better possible, by utilizing Zoom on your devices instead of your computers, you would not have to compromise functionality or vice versa. The features that are listed in this book can be used on all platforms, digital environments, screen sharing, etc. Zoom has ended your search if you are searching for a lightweight approach for video calling.

Not only is Zoom ideal for one-on-one meetings but community events of a hundred-plus participants can often be held with the Zoom. The built-in collaborative effort tools such as co-annotations, personal as well as community chat groups, shared calendars, and polling features can also be used. To put it another way, team meetings held with Zoom sound like in-person sessions. Zoom is the unchallenged pioneer in the field when it applies to video chat applications. Its mixture of in-depth functionalities, user design, and flexible pricing structure makes it a worthwhile addition to the software platform of any business. Just note to take maximum advantage of all of the functionality tools that are described in this book. If you do, you will feel all the benefits that Zoom gives.

When it comes to your family and friends, Zoom is a great way to get everyone together at the same time. You can host a meeting and chat over a glass of wine, organize a game for everyone to play, or create a quiz. The possibilities are endless.

Being a pro at hosting a video conference is important. But what's also important is leading the virtual meeting, especially if you are the host or team leader. However, as a participant, you should also actively participate and make the most out of your presence. Now that you have learned all the features that are available in Zoom, you are trained to use this service with expertise.

To sum it up, Zoom offers excellent support, basic and advanced features that enhance a successful video conference, impressive host and participant controls, thorough engagement, and, now, reliable security, making it a complete package.

With Zoom, you can thoroughly practice social distancing while achieving your daily meeting objectives, all virtually. And, as you have seen, this platform is straightforward and effortless to use. With multiple features and an efficient free plan, you are just a click away from downloading and using this wonderful service that will connect you to the world from the comfort of your home. So, whether it's a Pictionary game with your loved ones or an important business meeting, Zoom will assist you through it.

Have fun video-conferencing!

TEACHING

WITH ZOOM:

A Step-by-Step Beginners Guide to Zoom,
The Essential Software Worldwide for Teaching
and Learning Online. Bonus: 50 Tips for The
Effective Online Teacher.

ANDREW MURCEY

Introduction

There is no doubt that the world has greatly improved with the advent of all kinds of technological equipment. Communication has become so much easier that humans do not necessarily have to be together in a place to have a meaningful and productive conversation as well as transacting business in their day to day activities.

The world has been hit with the realization that technology and the internet are major keys to the survival of mankind, thus, the world is now moving to a dispensation whereby if you are computer illiterate, you will soon become obsolete and irrelevant.

The world presently is going through a major challenge that has never occurred in the history of the world, COVID 19 (Coronavirus). This pandemic has caused a lot of people to lose their jobs, economic meltdown, and schools and other social institutions being closed down. All in an attempt to curtail the spread of the virus which has led to the death of so many people in the world.

However, no matter how tough a problem is, there is a solution I will introduce to you a unique application called Zoom, and this application can connect business partners irrespective of their location. It can help students to continue with their studies right in their homes and allows people to socialize with each other despite the barriers the pandemic has brought.

However, it is important to know that there have been other video conferencing platforms such as Microsoft Teams, Skype for Business, etc. before Zoom and because of the features it possesses such as being user friendly, less costly, ability to record meetings, etc. it has taken over other applications and has become the leading application for video conferencing in the world today.

CHAPTER 1:

Setting Up and Organizing Your Meeting

A Zoom Meeting simply refers to a meeting that's been hosted through the Zoom application, and participants can partake via webcam or via phone.

DOWNLOAD THE APP:

To download the Zoom App (desktop or mobile app version), you can click here to go to the download page or Google https://zoom.us/download. Follow the steps and once downloaded on your computer, create an account, or log in with your Facebook or Google account. If you are using your computer or laptop, you will see this window below as soon as you enter.

Upon using a mobile app, an interface like this will pop up as soon as you enter.

For easier understanding, we are assuming that you are using the desktop version of Zoom.

If you are hosting a meeting, click on the 'New Meeting' option that is represented by the orange icon. You will enter an interface that enables you to change the settings according to your preferences.

CREATE A MEETING

Opening an account on the zoom platform is completely free, offers lots of amazing benefits, and solves your video interaction problems. No matter where you live, you will enjoy the stability of the platform and its web availability for your schedules and meetings. You must know how to create a meeting if you want to enjoy all the benefits of the platform.

Follow the steps below:

Download and open the platform's application to conduct and organize a meeting. When it launches, the following page lets you join, create a schedule, and share visuals. Select a new meeting.

If you wish to invite your co-workers or friends, select the invite control key. You can now copy and paste the URL invitation to share the invite through email. You can also utilize the email service to share the invite.To create a schedule for your meeting, click on the schedule. You should set the below steps in settings:

Topic

Select the topic field that you can input words, type the title.

Set your desired duration under and time to start

You can toggle off or on video for attendants and the admin whenever they wish to join

For audio settings, you can click on any of the following options, VoIP only, both, or telephone.

You can also mark the additional options for the meeting, whichever way you want. It is advisable to make attendants gain access by utilizing a pass-key and identity whenever they decide to join.

Select the calendar that you will utilize to build an invitation. You can copy the invite and share it on several calendar programs.

Click on the schedule control key if you want to copy the invitation and send it to other attendants.

HOST SETTINGS

Every admin in a video interaction can utilize the below attributes:

- Mute people
- Tell attendants to un-mute
- Stop intruding materials
- Tell individuals to start a video
- Stop attendants from sharing the visuals

- Modify the identity of people in the interaction

- Put attendants on hold

- Decide to start or stop the chime

- Lock video interaction

- Eradicate people from the conversation

MANAGE ATTENDANTS

You can control the attendants in a video conversation if you created it. Every attendant in the group can distribute different materials like videos and so on by default. You can also limit the number of people who can distribute files while the conversation is on utilizing the webinar platform.

Before you start managing individuals in a video interaction, it is essential to understand the order of attendants.

They are:

- You

- The admin (If that is not you)

- Contact information without names

- Muted and Un-muted attendants
- Only the admins can utilize the below attributes:
- Let attendants record locally
- Change the status of an attendant from member to co-host or host
- Authorize waiting room

To go through the attendant's list, select manage attendants inside the controls. Select the menu that drops down which you will find around the attendant's list or select pop out to divide the list through the page for meetings:

Hover on an attendant and select more for the below actions:

- Chat: Launch the page for the chat to get your messages to the admin.
- Halt video: It can stop the attendant's video so that they cannot start or launch their camera. Sometimes the attendant may not start their camera, but it will display the start control key.
- Designate host: You can utilize it to modify the status of people by making them, host. You can only have one.
- Designate co-host: It can also make the attendant a co-host, and there is no limited number for co-hosts.
- Enable record: It can let an individual stop or start recording the interaction locally. Attendants cannot cloud records.
- Rename: It gives uses the ability to modify the name of people that other attendants can see. You can utilize this feature in

only current meetings.

- Note: To modify your name that you can see, hover on it in the list of attendants and select rename. You must know that this change is not permanent, and if you want a permanent change, you should modify it in the profile. You can also place people in the waiting room while you utilize the available time to make preparations for the meeting. If you are hosting, then you should allow the waiting room so that it can appear for you to use it.

- On-hold: If you do not allow the waiting room, it will display the on-hold option where you can put people on hold.

- Remove: It helps the host remove attendants when they complete the project or at any time they desire. You should know that any participant that you remove cannot rejoin until you allow them again.

- It gives you access to allow and disallow the above options beneath the list of attendants.

- Invite: It lets you invite other individuals

- Mute and un-mute all: It gives you the power to un-mute or mute individuals in the current group.

- Let attendants un-mute themselves: It gives attendants the power to un-mute themselves to share an opinion

- Let attendants rename themselves: It gives the people the power to modify their identity that others can see whenever they desire.

- Lock meeting: You can use this attribute to lock every other attendant out of the meeting

- Join windows for a meeting: Merge the list of attendants with the original window for the interaction. Utilize this alternative if you divide the list of attendants from the initial one.

- To stop attendants from sharing the visuals, navigate to the settings, and select the arrow close to the share screen, and tap advanced sharing.

LINUX

Select manage attendants to show their list

Hover across an attendant and select more for the below actions:

- Designate host: modify the status of an individual from member to host.

- Designate co-host: Make individuals in the same group co-host. They have no limited number so that you can have as many as possible in one group.

- Record: It gives individuals the power to halt or start recording a meeting locally.

- Modify name: You can utilize this attribute to modify the name of individuals that other people in the same group can see. You can utilize this function for current meetings only.

- Note: You can also modify your name if you decide to perform the task, hover across it on the attendant's list, and tap rename. You must know that that altercation is not a permanent one, to modify your name permanently, you should perform that task in your profile.

- Halt video: You can utilize this attribute to stop the attendant's video connection, which makes it unlikely for them to start. If the individual is yet to start, it will display a start control key for you to control whenever you want.

- On-hold: You can utilize this one to put individuals on hold, withdraw them from the audio and video interactions. You have to allow the feature before you begin the interaction if you want to use the feature.

- Remove: You can use this attribute to remove individuals participating in the interactions. They cannot rejoin the meeting until you give them access again.

- It gives the authorization to turn off or on any of the above attributes below the list of attendants:

- Invite: It gives you the ability to invite anyone.

- You can utilize the play exit feature to play a sound anytime anyone wants to leave or join the interaction.

- Lock meeting: It gives you the power to lock everyone out of the conversation

CHROME

Select manage attendants to show the list of individuals involved in the interaction. Tap the menu that drops down to exit the list or select pop-out to divide the list from the page of the conversations.

Hover across an individual name and select more for the below actions:

- Chat: Launch this if you want to transfer texts to the admin.

- Halt video: You can utilize this attribute to halt the attendant's interaction, which will stop them from starting their camera on the platform. If you did not launch it, it would display a start control key for you to use whenever you wish to launch it.

- Designate host: Utilize this function to alter the position of an individual from member to host in the interaction.

- Designate co-host: Utilize this attribute to designate the co-host title to any individual in the same video communication. There is no limit to the number of them.

- Record: It gives attendants the power to halt or start a record of the conversation. Only admins can record via the cloud.

- Modify name: You can utilize this attribute to modify the names of individuals in the same conversation, modify names that others can see in the same group. You can perform this task on current meetings only.

- Note: To modify your name that you can see on display, you should hover across it in the list of attendants and select rename. You must know that the modification is not a permanent one, you can perform the task in the profile.

- Waiting room: It can help you place individuals in it so that you can utilize the rest of the time to prepare. You must allow the attribute to utilize it.

- On-hold: If you fail to allow the room feature, you use this one to keep the intruder on hold.

- Eradicate: You can use this feature to eradicate people from video interaction.

- It gives you the power to allow or disallow the actions beneath the list of people involved in the interaction by selecting more:

- Let attendants un-mute themselves: Anyone can now un-mute themselves in the video interaction with the use of this attribute. They can perform the task if they want to contribute to the conversation.

- Let people modify their names: People can now modify their names on display at their desired time with this attribute.

- Lock interactions: The feature gives you the power to lock everyone out of the video interaction while it is in progress.

- You can stop attendants from sharing the visuals by selecting the arrow around it and select sharing.

IOS

Select attendants to see the list of individuals involved in the video conversation.

Click on the individual name to control them.

- Designate host: Utilize this attribute to modify the position of anybody from member to host in the conversation.

- Record: It gives people in the same conversation the ability to

124 | P a g .

halt or start a record of the conversation. Only admins can record via the cloud.

- Waiting room: It can help you place individuals in it for some time so that you can utilize the rest of the time to handle essential things in the interaction. You must allow the attribute to utilize it.

- On-hold: If you fail to allow the room feature, you can use this one to keep the intruder on hold.

- Halt video: You can utilize this attribute to halt the attendant's video interaction, which will stop them from starting their camera on the platform. If you did not launch the video, it would display a start control key for you to use whenever you wish to launch it.

- Designate co-host: You can use this attribute to designate the title to any individual in the same video communication. There is no limit to the number of them.

- Modify name: You can utilize this attribute to modify the names of people in the same interaction, modify the name that other people in the same group can see. You can perform this task on current meetings only.

- Note: If you want to modify your identity that you can see, hover across it in the list of individuals involved in the interaction, and select rename. You must know that the modification is not a permanent one, you can perform the task in the profile.

- Remove: You can utilize this attribute to eradicate anyone from the interaction.
- You can hold conversations with attendants, invite, and perform several tasks with the options beneath the window.
- Lock interaction: The feature gives you the power to lock everyone out of the video interaction while it is in progress.
- Lock share: You can utilize this feature to stop attendants from sharing the screen.
- Let people in the same interaction chat: It gives you control over how people in the same video interact with one another.

ANDROID

Tap attendants to see the list of people involved in the video interaction.

Click on one person's name to control them.

- Designate host: Utilize this attribute to modify the position of anybody from member to host in the conversation.
- Designate co-host: You can use this attribute to designate the co-host title to any individual in the same video communication. There is no limit to the number of them.
- Waiting room: It can help you put people in it so that you can handle essential things at that time. You must allow the attribute if you want to utilize it.
- On-hold: If you fail to allow the room feature, you can use this one to keep the intruder on hold.

- Modify name: You can utilize this feature to modify the names of people. You can modify the name that other people in the same group can see. You can perform this task on current meetings only.

- Halt video: You can utilize this attribute to halt the attendant's video interaction, which will revoke their access to start their camera on the platform. If you did not launch the video, it would display a start control key for you to use whenever you want to launch it.

- Record: It gives people in the same interaction the power to halt or start a record of the conversation. Only admins can record via the cloud.

CHAPTER 2:

Desktop Video Conferencing

Log in to your zoom account.

Hover over the **Host a Meeting** button in the top right corner of the screen and choose one of the following options:

With video on

With video turned off

Just share the screen

Note: You can also quickly start a meeting from the desktop app by following the instructions below for mobile devices.

ADD PARTICIPANTS

Step 1: Start a new meeting in the Zoom desktop app.

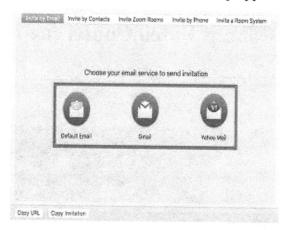

Step 2: Here, Zoom offers the option to copy URLs or to copy invitations. You can send them to the participants via SMS, email, or instant message.

Step 3: You can also email the meeting details directly via your preferred email client using the Zoom app.

Create an account and install Zoom on Desktop or Laptop

Go to **https://zoom.us/signup** and register by entering the data requested.

Now, select one of the two options:

- Manual registration; by entering your email and confirming the registration.

- Registration via the link from our Google or Facebook account (*recommended*)

REGISTRATION THROUGH GMAIL

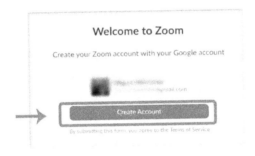

- The next step is to install the Zoom client on your computer. To perform this, go to **https://zoom.us/download,** and download "Zoom Client for Meetings."

Client download. Step 1

If we are downloading with the Google Chrome browser, we will see it in the lower-left corner. We wait until downloading is complete then we click on that.

Client download. Step 2

Once the program is open, we go to the Login section and log in again with our Google account, as we have done formerly.

Log in. Step 1 (you should see the English client)

Log in. Step 2 (you should see the English client)

Now, a pop-up window will open. We click "Open Zoom Meetings".

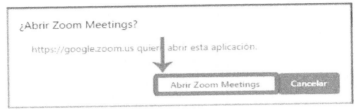

We already have our Zoom Client installed and ready to use.

CHAPTER 3:

The Benefits of Online Learning and Teaching

BENEFITS OF ZOOM

EASY SETUP

The platform is easy to use, and you can easily download, click, and set it up. It is the easiest video conferencing solution and the best innovation that has happened in the business world. It functions almost with just a click and can connect to meetings easily as well as help users hold interactions with customers. You can set up the platform with ease across different smartphones, gadgets, desktops, and also bring all the participants together seamlessly.

It has an excellent interface, rooms, and screen sharing for everyone. The platform also offers distinctive features, including training online, webinars, interactive meetings virtually, and so on. It also provides maximum and exceptional services and experience.

MINIMIZE THE COST OF TRAVELING

The idea of traveling to meet people can drain your time and money. The introduction of video conferencing makes holding and managing meetings with participants easy from several remote locations across the world. The platform has a feature that can make a person thousand miles away appear on a screen at your desired time and location, which cuts down the cost of traveling. Perform that task with a simple click while utilizing emails for pre-meeting arrangements or instant messaging. It gives users lots of benefits and satisfaction.

BINDS TOGETHER REMOTE EMPLOYEES

You can have workers all scattered in the various locations in the country or cities around you. The platform gives users the ability to connect workers. You can modify the application settings and use the video attribute for meetings with your workers. You can also utilize the attribute to check what your workers are doing and their locations. It is a useful platform for business owners as well as the workers, organizations, and lots more.

VIRTUAL BACKGROUNDS

The platform lets users replace the space with their favorite pictures. It is an attribute that you can utilize across all gadgets besides Android because it does not have high hardware demands. However, you can utilize the virtual background alternative, although the performance will differ. It is an essential attribute for remote workers or workers that work from home because it helps them connect with customers and co-workers easily via the video attribute. It also keeps the workspace organized and very easy to turn on and off. Users can modify backgrounds with just a few clicks.

TOUCH-UP APPEARANCE

It is an integrated attribute that can turn on easily on iOS and desktop. It is another one that android users cannot utilize because of high hardware standards. You can turn on and off the feature in the video settings. It includes a filter on the camera, smooth the lines, and removes every imperfection, which in turn gives the user a radiant look. It fine-tunes the user's face. It is an important feature for remote and online workers who have to attend early morning meetings.

WEB CLIENT

It is an alternative option for users who do utilize the zoom app. Users that wish to join meetings only can also utilize the web alternative. It is straightforward to utilize and easy to modify its settings. The users can also join the meeting through their browser, but it is not a default option.

So, if you're going to meet the admins or hosts for paid accounts, you should allow this option on the platform web portal.

MARKETPLACE

The platform has a marketplace where users can integrate several other software and tools, which makes it a unique tool to have for every business. It consists of different plugins that users can utilize for things like Salesforce, Slack, and various applications for business use. It performs various tasks beyond teleconferencing. Remote employees that spend lots of hours utilizing the zoom platform should also look into the marketplace and utilize it to the best of their capacity. It makes several tasks easy to perform, like managing, inviting, and organizing meetings.

RECORD MEETINGS

The platform comes with a recording attribute that users can utilize for meetings. It can capture video and record meetings happening on the zoom platform with just a few clicks. It is an essential attribute for the paid users who have an enterprise or business account. It also transcribes the records and uploads them to the cloud. Only an admin can turn the feature on and off, so you should make the right settings before you start the meeting. It is also a great feature for remote and online employees. They experience several technical problems, missing meetings, or want to go back to previous comments without strolling through the video to locate the perfect moment.

It is an attribute that users with a free account cannot utilize; it is available for paid users.

IT ALLOWS TELECOMMUTING

The attribute for video is an important tool for workers that work from home. If you have a timetable for your business and workers who work from home, you can eliminate a lack of communication in the group by video conferencing.

MEETING ORGANIZATION AHEAD OF TIME

Users can perform meetings without fumbling various applications for different reasons. It offers audio and video modes of communication as well as sharing screens. Although holding a meeting online is free and helps users minimize expenses and avoid restrictions, users can also organize meetings without limits. It gives different business the required speed and helps them evolve as the world moves.

Users also can give short notice on meetings before it starts, and every attendant will have no excuse to travel or change location. The only thing they need to do is give themselves the required freedom. You can create a schedule for video meetings in one minute and ensures that it runs immediately. It is a perfect advantage for users on a tight schedule.

HUMANIZE INTERACTIONS

It can humanize communications between attendants or conversations between employees. You must understand that a video is a collection of moving images that can be worth over one million words. The process of showing your face on the screen and looking at other attendants allows the introduction of body language charms, which is an advantage for business owners. Looking at a person while holding a conversation with them gives a good feeling and changes the nature of the interaction, it does not matter if it is a personal relationship or a business one.

ITEM DISPLAY

It is an advantage for business and organization who need to convince their customers. When they see the product live, it boosts their confidence and creates trust as well as convince the customer. With the utilization of the video attribute for conferencing, you can perform the task of writing on a board and displaying it so that everyone can see it. Display the most recent and latest items that you want to sell or make an introduction of recruits that will help your business grow. The platform gives users the chance to display items that they cannot put in a suitcase or convey from one location to another for meetings on the video platform.

INTERNET EDUCATION

There are different types of excellent courses that you will find on the internet and teachers that are ready to teach, but distance can become a problem. If you are a trainer or tutor that stays at a long distance from your students, utilizing zoom makes the process straightforward. It is an excellent concept of obtaining and distributing knowledge without facing any problems. Although you may not be present physically, that will not affect the task because it offers excellent communication quality. You can utilize multimedia tools, such as collaborative whiteboards and other collective tools. Another major benefit of zoom is that no matter the number of video calls attending, it does not diminish in quality.

PASSWORD PROBLEMS

Lots of people forget their password and ID regularly, but the platform offers a solution. You do not need the requirement of a login ID or pass-key to utilize the platform or worry about forgetting your details because, with few clicks, you are up running with it. It also eradicates the idea of voice blabbing and ensures that the person on the other side can hear whatever you say to them and vice versa. It is a straightforward and convenient platform to use.

EXCELLENT AUDIO AND VIDEO SERVICE

Checking the audio or video sounds and display quality is a great way to know which platform provides the best services, and the zoom platform is top of that category. The services that the platform offers stand out among its peers and provide excellent video services. Its quality does not diminish even in troubled locations that have low bandwidth or echo problems within its portals. It offers excellent performance and does not encounter any type of problems while in use even when the meeting attendants start joining the rooms.

ONLINE MEETINGS

Another great quality of the platform is the unquestionable quality of its audio and video services for several activities. The platform gives users the power to develop a URL and ID for the meeting and share it with every attendant. However, users must watch out for the usage of the central processing unit resources of the computer.

For example, during a video meeting, the processing unit can reach one hundred percent, which can be a downside because it will slow down the system and affect its performance. If you utilize the last versions of computers or at least two years old, you may not face any problems with your processing unit because it can manage HD graphics with ease, and you perform your task error-free.

SCALABILITY

You must understand that the zoom platform is expandable. It is a progressive solution, and unlike other platforms, it expands with an organization to manage the growing requirements. The ability to expand gives companies and business owners the ability to modify their skills of interaction amount their employees depending on their requirements and size.

VERSATILITY

The platform ensures that users enjoy a wonderful experience across every gadget because of its easy adaptability. It gives companies and business organizations the ability to manage every form of interaction. It does not matter if it is on a smartphone, desktops. It helps workers, managers, and customers create collaboration at any time and place with the use of the platform, whether in a car, office, or home.

PRICING

The zoom platform is affordable and has a great price structure for your business level and type. The pricing is a great tool for businesses and companies that want to advance their cooperation approach with little investment financially. It comes with four different plans with prices based on the number of hosts and the attributes it contains.

The plans include basic, business, professional, and enterprise. You will get a good value for your investment plan on the basics, and it is also a perfect choice for training online, sharing of the screen, inter-office meetings, and recording videos. The free version offers only forty minutes for every meeting, and it keeps each session short.

REDUCES EDUCATION COST

The video attribute for educational purposes saves a lot of cost for basic equipment for the process. Lots of institutions and schools in remote areas do not have the required funds to develop or enlarge educational buildings for various reasons.

Utilizing the feature is an excellent option for education in such areas.

It also gives the students another view of the world as well as build a new world for your pupils to see and learn things that they cannot learn in a regular class.

IMPROVES TUTOR TO PARENT CONNECTION

Lots of tutors have hopes of keeping close contact with parents, which the platform made easy with the video attribute that both parties can utilize to reach one another.

The concept of video meetings helps reduce misunderstandings between parents and teachers. Now tutors do not need to invite the parent to school meetings any longer.

They can now utilize the platform to perform that task. Parents can always join the video meeting from the tutor from any location in the world with an internet connection.

EXCELLENT SERVICE PROVISION ON SLOW NETWORKS

The platform offers wonderful services across gadgets with slow networks and can handle at least one hundred attendants at the same time.

It provides a good environment for webinars and business conferences.

The days of bandwidth problems are over because your data has a cloud server back up.

You must know that a maximum of one hundred attendants can share the screen and execute a meaningful interaction from a remote area.

IT PROVIDES A UNIFIED PLATFORM

Attendants can interact with one another whenever they want with the utilization of live chats during an interaction. It does not have a restriction on virtual or online meetings and webinars. So, anytime you want to distribute or share data or ask questions, you can perform that task with the live chat feature.

CHAPTER 4:

The Cons of Online Teaching

THE CONS OF ZOOM

Zoom is a great platform for meetings on the market today. It provides a regular experience for users and consists of wonderful tools that functions with each other optimally. It is a straightforward and reliable software for video conferencing and different other businesses.

Users utilize the platform for several tasks, which include online meetings, interaction with text via groups, and video communication. It offers excellent screen sharing and audio experience across gadgets like Windows and the likes. It is affordable and can satisfy several businesses ' needs. However, zoom comes with several cons. The expansion of services to the education and the business healthcare sector ensured that the zoom platform reached its potential peak. Although the platform is the best for your business requirements, it also has its limitations, which can be a disadvantage to its users.

Lots of researchers have found several disadvantages of the platform, which includes infringement of privacy policy and the like.

Below are a few cons of utilizing the zoom platform:

EXPENSIVE

Utilizing the zoom platform incurs additional costs because there the platform comes with add-ons. You can remove that option on the basic plan level, which will make it less expensive. When you begin the addition of the extras, the price continues to go up with every inclusion.

DIFFERENT PLAN PATTERNS

The different platform types of plans are a benefit, but when it becomes too much, and you hardly know which one to pick. You might even think of customizing your plan.

The platform comes with different types of issues for different plans and can, in turn, send customers who just want a basic plan to enjoy their services away.

SLOW CUSTOMER SERVICES

A representative can take about two to three days to give replies about solutions to a problem and how to fix them whenever you contact them. It can be very frustrating and can put your business at risk.

It is really hard to find an organization, business, or sector without the utilization of the zoom platform to conduct their online meetings and video interactions among employees so you can understand why they have service delay problems.

INTRUSIONS

The zoom platform has a high vulnerability to cyber-attacks and hackers. Black hats can forcefully get passwords and take control over virtual and online meetings as well as post demeaning or offensive content to destabilize business activities.

Fortunately, they came up with several strict measures to control the situation and remove every security problem. Another rising problem that can lead to the loss of users on the platform is the attack from cybercriminals on zoom users. It can cause a significant backlash, and the platform can lose lots of users at the same time.

LINKS TO CHINA

There have been different accusations about the selling of data and information to another social media platform, and also reports linking the platform to the Chinese servers.

At some point in time, the chief executive officer at Zoom, Eric Yuan, made an admission of mistakenly routing calls through a server belonging to the Chinese to avoid the congestion of networks. It is a rising problem for Americans using the platform because of its security problems.

CHAPTER 5:

Preparing for Class

Zoom was developed with creativity. Now, if you make confident important choices and familiarize yourself with the application before welcoming students into an informal conference. Zoom's free edition can provide you with the best performance and features while holding a Class. Remember to coach the students to have Zoom activated. Students preparing to attend Zoom meetings from a Laptop or computer will also access the application from the Zoom website.

PREPARATIONS

- Get to learn the controls on the server.
- Catch up on managing a quick Zoom meeting.
- Sign up to work out.
- Check the recording and the audio.
- Visit zoom.us/test to confirm the internet, video, and audio connections.
- When there are several meeting participants in the same area, only one person can enter the conference with audio to prevent suggestions.
- Find the source of light.
- Make sure a source of light should be in front of you and not behind you.

SCHEDULE CLASS

Zoom provides webinars and conferences. All formats help you to communicate with students, although some variations do occur. To pick the style that fits better for you, choose the Zoom flowchart or webinar/meeting comparison chart. Go to the Navigation section to the Zoom feature, press Plan a New Conference and obey the directions.

1. Enable your device with the Zoom Windows software.
2. Tap at the upper left on "Back".
3. Tap "Schedule".
4. Enter all related information such as day, year, subject, etc.

5. Select your favorite digital calendar (Google Calendar is perfect if you have got Mail or email accounts), and you will be brought to a page with your Zoom connection.

6. You may give the connection to your students in the meeting scheduler of your online calendar.

When applicable, choose regular meetings such that the URL can stay the same over the course. Try to place a positive name on your conferences. When you intend on learning:

- Meetings of the course occur inside the platform of the Zoom course.
- Recordings can be made accessible automatically via the course page.
- The course meetings can be separated from other conferences.
- Planned meetings often serve as activities for Calendar class participants.

For unplanned events, simply use your meeting ID and official Zoom URL. Such gatherings won't have the advantages mentioned earlier, so cannot be hosted by someone else.

PLAN ROLES

Assigning specific tasks to the students may be an efficient means of coordinating group practice. Often certain students take too much accountability for the activity of a community, while others may be hesitant to commit to the activities of the group. Assigning responsibilities helps to spread liability among group members and guarantees transparency for the involvement of all students. As students practice various roles, they have the chance to develop a wide range of competencies.

The most commonly needed positions for group work include facilitator, planner, and organizer, timekeeper, and issue manager. You would want to create notes of what it feels like when the job is done well when it is not done well. Ask the students to comment on their perspectives operating in communities in writing or solving issues. Students might still have suggestions for different assigned positions.

When you appoint someone else to handle facets of digital rooms, you will have a less challenging classroom managerial experience. Try requesting one supervisor or student to track the conversation and one to assist their peers with difficulties with technology. Formal identification of alternate hosts may also be created. This way, you will focus on giving lectures and offer some additional technical skills to the students.

ENHANCE STUDENT'S SENSE OF COMMUNITY

If everybody reveals their faces through their webcam, the feeling of presence is strengthened. Suggest asking students to click on film as a core component of attendance, because if you can see them, it becomes simpler to communicate with the class, so students are more willing to pay care because they realize they are on display. Train students even about how to turn to the view of the Gallery (this is the

perspective where everybody is equally accessible to one another).
Suggestions to connect with your students:

- Make eye contact with the camera.
- Mute mics in case you do not participate.
- Find the illumination! Make sure a bright light is in front of you and not behind you.
- Talk in a conversational way-you does not need to talk up.
- Read on to operate a seamless meeting in Zoom for further information.

A good sense of community can boost the class online and lead to student achievement. The culture can be improved if you take action to keep it protected from harassment or disturbance. A few approaches to meet such targets are here:

- Introduce yourself with the safe Zoom Meetings setups and guidance.
- Using the regional meeting configuration and in-meeting guidelines to ensure the class is attended only by enrolled learners and invited visitors.

MANAGE TECHNICAL PROBLEMS

For every video conferencing program, the three most important technological problems are:

- Members could not see.
- Members could not hear.

- External noise and mic problem.

You can overcome technical issues by hosting an online training meeting for reduced stakes, with the primary aim of signing in, troubleshooting technological issues, and getting accustomed to the Zoom application. Get in your meeting early enough to sort out technical problems. Provide a contingency strategy in case of unknown complications or challenges. Students are informed of the backup plan in advance so that if technical issues arise, they can stay on task.

Know how to address these problems by troubleshooting issues. Try communicating with your community the Participant's Guide for enhancing Your Zoom Performance. It is recommended to host an online discussion experience with low-stakes introductory meetings, whose primary purpose is to have an entire team login, diagnose problems technical issues, and get used to Zoom functionality.

CREATE A TEACHING AGENDA

Prepare for a simultaneous training session online much as you would prepare for an in-person meeting. Discuss the plan with students in advance, and students do have a good understanding of how the curriculum will proceed, what will be discussed and the events they will compete in. Periodically review web behavior and student aspirations, or recommend providing the "good management" guide detailing goals.

Plan for a concurrent session of the course much as you would prepare for knowledge gives the lesson. Here is a testing agenda for a simultaneous sixty-minute instructor meeting to share your agenda with students in advance, so they know what is coming:

- Make students reflect on a problem before joining the digital classroom and write their answers on the whiteboard.

- Using the polling method to ask a question that includes and decides personal significance for the Mini-reading subject.

- Link computer launches PowerPoint and offers mini-readings. To mark the PowerPoint slides, use the Annotation functionality in Zoom.

- Render the survey issue provisionally.

- Assign students to separate breakout spaces, chat for ten minutes, and develop a shared Google Report.

- Ask each party to appoint a delegate, to sum up, the main points of their debate.

- Ask students to ask questions if they are always puzzled.

- Clear up misunderstandings found in the muddiest point of the conversation.

- Summarize the session's tasks, set goals for the follow-up events, and achieve them.

RECORD CALLS FROM ZOOM AS A VIDEO

Zoom lets you record video phone calls. And you need permission to do so. The host of the meeting would have to require recordings in environments. It is worth testing the settings of your account to ensure recording is allowed before you start.

1. Sign in to your account at Zoom.

2. Tap to view Account Settings / Configurations.

3. Navigate to the Registration tab and click Video Recording.

4. It is worth noting that Zoom administrators will allow recording for all users or groups. There is more guidance here regarding recording settings.

5. To record a meeting with Zoom, you need to choose whether to use the local or Cloud option.

6. Local means that you store the video file on your device or in another storage area yourself. Zoom saves the video for you in cloud storage using Cloud, which is for paid subscribers only.

7. When the call to zoom begins, you will see a choice to record at the bottom of the screen. Clicking that lets you log in the Cloud or locally.

8. If you can't see the recording feature, check your web app settings (under My Meeting Settings) or have your account administrator activate it. You can transfer the recording files to a computer or stream them from a browser.

9. You can also see during the meeting which participants are recording the meeting, and when the meeting is recorded, it will also be told to those at the meeting. When the call is over, Zoom will turn the recording automatically into a functional MP4 video format.

RECORD YOUR CLASS

If somebody has a technological problem, you can offer them further access to the course work. You should report the class session to counter this. Record on the web, not on your desktop: Recording in the cloud is easy because you will access both a video URL and an online transcribed clip.

Begin recording in the appropriate style: Once you start recording, the recording interface is focused on your vision. Note: to swap presentations and turn to an active speaking view rather than a gallery (or do not use the camera or anything), or you will be overlaid in the clip over the upper right corner.

While recording your class, keep in mind certain things;

- Let the students know that you will be recording the class.
- Give students a choice to silence their audio when filming and switching off their camera.
- When meetings are captured in the cloud, and you use a module, the recordings can be located right in the PC.
- Such records could be done to specific preservation procedures than other documentation of class sessions.
- For advice about where to place the recordings, and how to show them to your students, contact your local university development help.

CHAPTER 6:

Zoom Features

To decide whether or not Zoom will work for you, it is important to know what Zoom can and cannot do. In this section, I will be going over the key features of the software so you will have a better understanding of what you can do with it. The features that you will be able to use will vary on whether you are using the free version of Zoom, or if you are using one of the subscription-based services. As of this writing, there is the free version and three subscriptions (paid) versions that you can use, each with their own set of features.

As you might have figured out by now, you can use Zoom to host meetings and webinars which is a fancy word for a web seminar. While you are running a meeting or webinar, you will be able to use some or all of these features to enhance their functionality.

Here is a listing of some of the more commonly used features.

- Individual and group chat messages: This allows you to send messages to other users participating in your meeting or webinar.

- Screen sharing: Allows you so share all of your screen or just a certain program with other participants, so they can see what you are working on.

- Screen annotation: Lets you mark up your screen to make notes or highlight certain aspects of your presentation.

- Whiteboard: This can be used just like a whiteboard you would have on the wall in a conference room where you can draw diagrams and write notes that can be shared with everyone in your meeting.

- Keyboard and mouse control: If you would like to give another participant control of the mouse and keyboard on your computer, you can use this option.

- Custom invitations and scheduling: When you create a meeting or webinar you can send out invitations to others and also have it added to various calendars, such as Outlook and Google.

- Meeting recording: If you need to review your meeting after it is complete you can have Zoom record it later and save it on your computer or in the cloud.

- Breakout rooms: This feature allows you to divide up your participants into separate rooms so they can collaborate on their own, or with specific people.

- Video effects: If you want to add a little fun to your meeting, you can use video effects such as background scenery for your meeting.

- Templates: When making webinars, you can create templates that can be reused so you do not have to go through the setup process from scratch each time.

Mobile device support: Zoom can run on a variety of smartphones and tablets so you can have your meetings from just about anywhere.

ENGAGING STUDENTS USING DIFFERENT FEATURES

No one likes sitting through a normal classroom lecture for sixty minutes, and the reality that you have all the teachers there and present does not influence such a class session structure. You may use the Zoom functions to direct various kinds of interactive tasks. Such tasks provide flexibility to break up a long-class session and provide diverse forms of communicating themselves.

CHAT

Using the chat platform will promote interaction by encouraging students to connect, rather than only listen, with the live operation. Also, Chat has advantages over conventional classroom: Get vast quantities of replies to a question right away, then use those answers in need or save them for later. See just where the students feel on a specific topic of discussion, advising them who to contact next.

Think about when, or where to allow students to talk. Are you happy with feedback during the class in chat, for example, or just at specific points? If you have a supervisor that can delete comments, you can require students to chat on an ongoing basis; otherwise, you can promote its usage at distinct times. Chat enables posts to be submitted to the whole community or another user. If you want to hold the record, you may access the complete chat history of the lesson.

For students, chatting can be unbearable. It is advised that you provide this form of interaction as an alternative, but not all students need it. Even chat can be challenging to track when you are still attempting to lecture.

Here are some tips for Chat:

- Provide a student or supervisor supervising the conversation so that you can concentrate on teaching.
- Recreate live posting on twitter of guest lectures as a way to gather questions and answer them at the end of the meeting.
- Select one student to track the conversation when they come in and to compile queries.

- Create a simulated team, where a selected community of students collaborates to solve a question or address an issue.

- The other students respond via the chat communications channel to contributions with their fellow students.

- Invite students to record questions as small groups during your classes and invite one student to address them for community discussion.

SCREEN SHARING AND ANNOTATION

Zoom provides simple annotation resources that can be used to direct or illustrate an idea to students. Use such resources by choosing the choice Annotate while viewing the display. Computer annotations were not open to those of screen readers. When you are utilizing this tool, make sure to follow best practices for open presentation: explain what you are doing when you are doing it (for example, "drawing a huge red ring around the registration form on this new website").

Sharing the screens is very important to show to your students to enhance your teaching skills and your students' learning ability.

You will share the computer screen with anyone at the Zoom meeting using this icon of screen sharing. Sharing a screen with Zoom is simple; all you have to do is press on the "Share Screen" link at the bottom of your conference. You will then press on the device you would like to display. Its modern technology and infinite functionality which help students in their classroom are becoming more efficient and imaginative.

POLLING

Engagement in a virtual class is a core aspect of student performance. Try integrating polling functionality into difficult concepts to improve student interest with your online course.

Polling enables students to share their experiences and communicate with each other, and often tells coordinators about the students in the class and encourages them to set the stage for a positive segment further.

Polls are simple to set up and then use and will bring value to an online course.

A teacher is provided with several ways to incorporate this practice into Zoom. Set up polling ahead of time and start them in your class meeting.

For an online course, surveys are an essential method, as they can:

- Link students in the classroom so that they can express their views on different topics.
- Be more interactive in introducing a topic or action.
- Give useful information on the readiness and progress of the students.
- Help guide and concentrate students on their education.

NON-VERBAL FEEDBACK

Significant feedback on assignments promotes analytical thought, proactive practice, and establishes relationships between teacher and student, which are vital in an online setting.

Although feedback helps evaluation, improvement, and enhancement of results, it often improves student enthusiasm when they believe that the teacher is involved in their progress.

To encourage students to connect with the coaching staff without disturbing the class, enable the non-verbal input function for your meetings.

Check-in with the students regularly to answer any non-verbal suggestions.

This app also helps you to handle vocal input, since students will be told to use the "lift hand" function to signal when they want to talk. Need to make students quiet before you order them to remove outside input from the room.

BREAKOUT ROOMS

Breakout Rooms encourage you to divide the meeting into several meetings, in a live classroom environment, comparable to community breakout sessions.

Students should create their social groups and would promote further interaction.

You will use the versatility of the breakout rooms in Zoom to help students perform collective learning.

As the teacher, when it is time to rebuild, you can enter the breakout rooms, relay notices to the breakdown rooms, and finish the breakdown session.

ZOOM FUNCTIONALITIES FOR TEACHING ONLINE

We have seen some of the most interesting features of Zoom. Now I will go into detail into where its potential lies.

1. GROUP CLASSES

Sessions can host as many participants as if you were in the classroom. You see and hear the students. You can see their faces as you explain, so you know if they are following you or are lost.

2. LIVE CLASSES

Giving live sessions is something unmatched. Students are connected and share the virtual classroom with their classmates. The camaraderie and a feeling of closeness are generated despite the distance.

3. DEFERRED CLASSES

If any student is unable to attend life, you can see the recording of the class. Also, if the teacher can't give the class for whatever reason, you can record it earlier and have it play when the time comes.

4. TUTORING

A close and direct way to have a tutorial with each of your students. Audiovisual communication lowers barriers and helps to empathize. A much more natural way of communicating than a phone call.

5. SHARE PRESENTATIONS

Excellent and demands utility for every self-respecting teacher. What would a virtual class be without its PowerPoint or PDF presentation? You can also share the screen to show a photo or an exercise.

6. SHARE VIDEOS

The possibility of screen sharing opens up a range of possibilities, among which is the sharing of audiovisual content, such as an interview with an expert in a certain subject, a documentary, or an educational video.

7. VIRTUAL WHITEBOARD

This functionality allows us to turn our screen into a whiteboard. The advantage is that here there is no chalk to stain you and that erasing the board is a matter of clicking.

This is very useful to solve exercises and make explanations with graphic support.

8. RAISE YOUR HAND

The student can raise his hand as if it were a face-to-face class. The teacher will receive a rather subtle warning on their screen. In this way, you will know that there is a student who has a question and who it is.

You can continue with your explanation or stop to solve it.

9. CREATE SURVEYS

A very cool feature to make the lesson more enjoyable and participatory. The trainer can ask questions so that the students answer and validate their knowledge.

10. CHAT

This is a very interesting functionality and a double-edged sword. It is interesting because it increases the interaction between the whole classroom; It is dangerous if private chat is activated since students will be able to write to each other without the teacher knowing it and they will be distracted.

CHAPTER 7:

The Zoom Whiteboard

T he Zoom Touch Whiteboard screen is an amazing feature for presentations and teaching. It has a tools area where you can select text, drawing tool, spotlight eraser, etc., there are many tools there that you can use on your whiteboard for your presentations.

Using the whiteboard within a zoom meeting is incredibly useful but there were a couple of things that we need to be aware of and a couple of settings you need to be aware of so everything can run smoothly.

HOW TO USE A WHITEBOARD

- Log into Zoom
- Join a meeting

- Tap meeting settings

- Tap on the Share Screen button

- Tap Whiteboard

- Tap Share

- The drawing/writing tools will come up automatically, but you can hide or show them.

WHITEBOARD DRAWING METHODS

There are two types of drawing methods you can use to annotate on the whiteboard after starting a session in a zoom meeting for Touch. They are:

Free Form: This is just like freehand sketching. Zoom will not smooth out the sketches or convert the drawings to shapes. They will just remain as you drew them.

Smart recognition drawing: In this mode, the zoom will smoothen out your lines and convert your drawings to shapes automatically after you sketch them on the touchscreen monitor.

These drawing methods are also available when annotating on a participant's shared screen.

SHARING WHITEBOARD ON IPHONE

- Log in to Zoom
- Host a meeting
- Click Share Content in the meeting settings, it's at the top-right side of the screen.
- Click on Whiteboard.
- The annotations tools will appear by default however you can click the pen tool to hide and show them.
- Click Stop Share when you are done.

SHARING WHITEBOARD ON ANDROID

- Log in to Zoom
- Host a meeting
- Click Share Content in the meeting settings, it's at the top-right side of the screen.
- Click on Whiteboard.
- Click the pen tool icon to show the annotation tools.

- Click the pen tool icon to hide the annotation.
- Click Stop Share when you are done.

There are two functions here that are very specific to this whiteboard.

- You can enable and disable the participant's annotations.
- You can also show the names of the annotators. You will see that all their names will show up on your screen as they are making their annotations.

This is incredibly useful if you are doing a collaborative project and you do want them to annotate and add their information to your whiteboard.

CHAPTER 8:

The Best Way to Make Use of Zoom Virtual Backgrounds

I'm going to show you an amazing tool and a feature called Virtual Backgrounds. This feature works most efficiently with a green screen setup but that's optional. This feature gives you access to go through and select default backgrounds, ranging from a night-city view from a penthouse, a beach in the Maldives, or an empty executive conference room if that's what you want.

However, you can upload your custom image or video as a virtual background.

When you start your meeting and it opens up the Zoom application.

- Click your profile picture
- Click Settings
- This is where you select your camera, and you also choose the virtual background.
- Then choose the virtual background.
- If you have your green screen setup, click on the "I have a green screen" so that Zoom can automatically adjust your background.
- If you don't have a green screen setup, just make sure that your background is of solid color like red, blue, yellow, black, orange, purple, green.

To have your mac updated to the latest OS,

- Go to the Apple menu at your computer's home page.
- Click on System Preferences.
- Click on Software Update.
- Click on Update Now to install the latest update.

To have your non-mac computer updated to the latest OS,

- Go to the System menu at your computer's home page.
- Click on System Preferences.
- Click on Software Update.
- Click on Update Now to install the latest update.

If your computer does meet those requirements then you will be able to simply click on any of the default images. Some of them are default images that Zoom gives you.

You can get your virtual backdrops from royalty-free sites such as pixabay.com or you can buy from shutterstock.com. These are places where you can find background images that you can then just import, and how you do that is,

- Click here on the little plus sign
- It will ask you to add a virtual backdrop.
- Look for the image on your computer and add it in

Again, you cannot be wearing green when you are attempting to use green screen technology, so don't be wearing any green including green accessories. You can buy a green screen setup from shops near you or online. If your computer meets the requirements, then you're good to go and it's that simple.

Also, avoid wearing clothes and accessories that are the same color as your virtual background.

VIRTUAL BACKGROUND ON IPHONE AND IPAD

To use the virtual background on your iPhone or iPad. Just follow the following instructions.

- Login to your zoom account.
- Join a meeting.
- Click the More tab by the bottom right of the meeting page.
- Click on the Virtual Background button.
- Select a background from the default drops provided by zoom.
- Or click on the plus sign to upload your images to use.

- Click Close after selecting your preferred virtual background to go back to the meeting.
- To turn off the background, just open the virtual background options and choose option None.

ENABLING VIRTUAL BACKGROUND FOR ZOOM GROUP

To allow this feature for all members of a specific group, follow the steps below

- Sign in to zoom web portal as an administrator with authorization to edit user groups.
- Tap on Group Management.
- Tap on the name of the group, then click on the Setting button.
- Go to the Virtual Background option on the meeting button and verify that the setting is enabled.
- If you want this setting to be compulsory for all users in the group, then click Lock to make it so.

However, bear in mind that the users must sign-out of their Zoom Desktop Client and sign in again for this setting to take place.

CHAPTER 9:

Interactions with the Students

When teaching online, it is equally important to build a positive relationship with each of your students. Doing this can be more challenging than in an in-person classroom because you can't immediately see how each student is reacting to what is happening. Body language plays an important role in communicating with others.

Interaction and communication are crucial in online teaching. Speaking effectively is one of the problems that online tutors face. Often, we create a beautiful course that is captivating and interesting, but teaching the course is a big issue.

If you are already an online tutor, you can also apply these tricks in your online teaching. Let us look at them one after the other.

COMMUNICATE RESPECTFULLY

Take note of this when communicating with your students. Respect is the pillar of effective communication, especially with students.

While sitting on the computer, it is easier to forget that there are students on the other side. Sometimes, students might ask you provocative questions.

You might be pushed to reply to the student in a thought-provoking manner. But it is wrong.

Always pause and meditate before you lash out to the student.

Avoid character attacks or unnecessary accusations. If you disagree with your student on particular issues, look for a way to address what he is saying, rather than attacking the student.

While teaching, most notably during live videos, you will encounter a situation where the student is not paying attention. Sometimes, you encounter a situation where the student will ask you questions that you have answered over and over again.

What is left for you, is to calm down and address the situation.

Like I said earlier, think about it as if you are teaching your students offline. It will help you to handle some issues.

TIPS ON HOW TO BUILD A RELATIONSHIP EVEN AT A DISTANCE

Many teachers begin their in-person classroom teaching with some ice-breaker activities. Such activities can help you to better understand each of your students which can lead to the building of a positive relationship between you and your students.

Here are some tips on how to further strengthen relationships:

MAKE USE OF A TONE THAT IS COURTEOUS AND HONEST

This involves choosing words that are appropriate to the situation. Avoid using inflammatory words, which can infuriate the students or cause an emotional response.

FOCUS ON WHAT YOU ARE TEACHING

Avoid things that can distract you when you are teaching your students online. Sometimes, you see teachers walking out of camera view to attending to some needs and returning later. Most of those actions can infuriate the students. So, once you walk into the view of your camera, focus on what you want to teach.

APOLOGIZE FOR YOUR MISTAKES

Learn to apologize when you make a mistake. Some emergency might come up, and you will have to end the class abruptly. Apologize for ending the class and give the students tangible reasons for your need to end the class.

It is very disrespectful to end a live class without giving a reason.

USE CLEAR AND CONCISE WORDS

When you are communicating with your students, be as clear as possible. It will help your students to understand you very well. Before you say something, give thought to what you want to say. Think about how your students will respond to such questions. Do not confuse your students with unclear sentences.

MAKE YOUR COMMUNICATION PERSONAL

One of the significant ways you can do that is by having a class discussion from time to time. In the class discussion, every student will be allowed to interact with each other. It will boost the confidence of the students.

START AND END WITH KEY POINTS

In other to ensure that your students will understand your lesson, reiterate critical points at the start and end of the course. Another way to do that is by adding a footnote at the end of the course. The note will serve as a reminder to the students.

CHAPTER 10:

How to Build Empathy at a Distance

P utting yourself in the shoes of another person is known as empathy which can be a tremendous help in establishing a bond with your students.

When you respond with a paraphrase, it is important that your comments, either verbally or not-verbally, do not place a value judgment on your response. A paraphrase should be a neutral statement that captures the intent of what the student is saying or their related feelings. Even when we disagree with what a student is saying, it is important to reflect on how he sees the situation, rather than attempting to impose our values on him. The exception to this might be when a student is providing information that relates to the breaking of a law (which necessitates you informing the appropriate authorities).

Paraphrases should be shorter than the initial response from the student. As the student talks to you, focus on the key thoughts or feelings of what he is saying to use in your paraphrase.

As you paraphrase, attempt to keep the ownership of what is being said on the student. You might respond with statements such as "If I'm hearing you correctly, you are saying…" or "I think what you're saying to me is…"

When you're attempting to reflect a feeling, attempt to use exact references to what the student has said regarding his feelings. Frustration, fear, anger, and confusion are common feelings a student might be talking about, but your interpretation of how he is feeling might be quite different than his perception. This is an area where you might provide a short paraphrase of what he is telling you and follow it up with an open-ended question along the lines of "What feelings are you experiencing as a result of this?"

After you paraphrase, it's critical to wait for the student's response back to you. The response should either confirm what you have said or disagree with what you have said. This can occur non-verbally by the student nodding his head in agreement or shaking his head in disagreement. It can also occur verbally when a student says something like "Exactly," or "You're right!" (and when you get either of these responses, celebrate in your mind that you are on the right path to understanding the student). If the student disagrees with your paraphrase, this can still contribute to understanding. The student will likely still realize that you are trying to understand what he is saying. You can then follow this up with something along the lines of "Help me to better understand what you are telling me then. What would be a better way for me to summarize what you are saying?"

After some time, or at the end of your conversation, you should summarize what you have been talking about. A summary might simply be described as two or three paraphrases linked together to provide an overview. As before, don't conclude your interview until the student confirms the correctness of your summary.

As stated earlier, paraphrasing contributes to empathy, a skill that can be learned by your students as you model it. Empathy may be one of the most important "soft" skills for developing positive relationships with other people. It may also be one of the most important classroom skills to develop a welcoming learning environment.

CHAPTER 11:

How to Use Zoom for Webinars

D ue to the pandemic, large gatherings beyond a certain number as well as business meetings, workshops, conferences, informative symposiums have been halted This had led to a paradigm shift and innovative ways have been introduced via Zoom thereby helping organizations, businesses [both large, small and medium enterprises, government parastatals to still undertake important meetings, training, symposiums online.

Webinars are invaluable in galvanizing a group of people that can't be together for the sake of workshops, impromptu meetings. It makes it possible for such activities to occur like they were all there.

Zoom has taken the lead in making these activities possible

WHAT IS A WEBINAR?

It's noteworthy to understand what a Webinar is; A Webinar refers to an online event where a speaker or more addresses a large audience on a particular topic of interest. Webinars give the host a level of control over such meetings via enhanced features.

Zoom webinar services can accommodate a 100-10000 audience. To activate your webinar service, you have to choose any of the zoom plans that you can afford and buy the webinar add-on to be able to subscribe to the webinar services. The zoom plan subscribed to determines the number of people that can attend the meeting

HOW TO HOLD A ZOOM WEBINAR

Having been licensed by Zoom, you can proceed to put your webinar in shape

Highlight the Webinar option in the Personal section of the Zoom icon, schedule a webinar button will pop up, select it

After that, fill in the topic for the webinar, elucidate what the webinar would entail, and signify when it will take place.

Interestingly, there's room for webinars occurring periodically, to get this done, click on the Recurring webinar bar, you then get to decide how often it will occur, the time it should take place, and also the date when it should end.

Additional checkmates can be introduced to streamline your audience. Having a period when your audience is expected to register before a set deadline and then given a password that grants them access to the webinar via the specified gadget, you also reserve the right to decide if the host/hosts can be seen during the webinar.

Furthermore, you can choose to create opportunities for questions and answers, if the option is enabled, attendees can get to see the questions, or it's made anonymous

To access the webinar Q&A settings, scroll to Webinar Option, click Q&A, and select Schedule

Alternative hosts have the permission to oversee meetings in your stead once they receive the link via a notification email however scheduling of meetings is your responsibility.

You can save this event to your Google calendar using the confirmation page. Towards the end of the confirmation page, you'll see an invitation bar that enables you to incorporate your panelists, feed them with details of the event that are disseminated to your attendees

From the email settings tab, you can determine the arrangement of emails to be sent to panelists and attendees before the event as reminders and as follow-up messages when the event is over.

You can decide to add flavor to your zoom webinar by adding colorful logos/designs to invitations sent to your attendees

REGISTERING ATTENDEES FOR ZOOM WEBINAR

Under Invite Attendees, click edit. You can ask your attendees to register using a form or submit their biodata {name and email address}. Approval can be done manual or otherwise automatic

Your choice of registration should depend largely on your intention, if you have plans to follow your attendees up after the webinar/do a survey, you can ask questions that will enable you to know more about them

How to register attendees for a Zoom webinar with JotForm

After setting up your webinar, locking down your co-hosts, it remains pertinent to get people to attend your event; hence you have to make sure attendees signing up do this without glitches

This is where Jotform comes in. It provides a glitch-free way of extracting data from attendees and it enables you to fashion the questions to suit your taste. It also allows you to sell your company value/culture through making customized designs in the form off course although templates are available, and it gives you the leverage to determine to an extent the response intended from your attendees

You can ask attendees to provide certain information when they register for your webinars, such as their job title, the name of their company, the number of employees, or their address.

During the registration, attendees can be asked for relevant information such as their occupation, company name, address; it can be made compulsory before attendees sign up for your webinar

Once the attendees complete the filling of the form, they are verified automatically. This form can also be linked to several online payment platforms hence registration fees can be collected for these webinars. There are no hidden charges; hence only standard charges apply to these payment platforms are deducted

If you chose the option of automatic approval, you can just take a chill pill and watch your attendee base surge but if you opted for manual approval, you have to log in to the zoom app and manually approve those that filled the Jotform

HOW TO ENABLE REGISTRATION FOR A ZOOM WEBINAR

To ensure people register, enable the register bar which is found under the personal section of your zoom portal and the webinar tab, this cannot be overemphasized and should be credence even before data collection, however, if the webinar has already been scheduled, it can be edited by selecting the already archived webinar under the 'Upcoming webinar' tab

Towards the end of the page, select Edit this Webinar, this takes you back to the menu where you can enable registration ab-initio.

CHAPTER 12:

Tips for Getting the Most Out of Zoom Video Conferencing

Z oom video conferencing can be a staple of modern communications, but the technology is still young enough to make room for improvement. A video conference can be either the best thing on Earth or one of the most uncomfortable things you can imagine, depending on how you plan.

Zoom is the best video conferencing solution, but it's just one piece of the video conference experience. To make participants feel as if they meet face-to-face, the entire process needs to be seamless.

You'll need the right hardware and, maybe, a minor shift in the way you use your computer to make your interactions with others come alive. If you are using a tablet or cell phone, hardware options may not have as much versatility as desktop computers, but there are still things you can do to improve your experience. Let's look at the elements required for an excellent video gathering experience.

The following tips will help ensure that you conference in an enjoyable, constructive manner whenever you talk:

DRESS FOR THE OCCASION

The dress is another significant aspect. It is better to clothe yourself absolutely – otherwise, as one CEO did, you could unintentionally show boxers underneath the suit and tie. Dress up with an emphasis on convenience, rather than sophistication, when in doubt. Video conferences can be pretty long and the more comfortable you're in your clothes, the more attractive the opportunity.

FOCUS ON HOUSE FURNITURE

Furniture is essential both when you're just a single participant and when organizing a video conference for a group. The chair and table should be ergonomically set up to enable natural, comfortable seating. In group settings, the focus should be on oval tables rather than the classic, long conference tables.

INVEST IN A GOOD CAMERA

Healthy hardware is an absolute must in all situations. Cameras that are built-in the laptops are a poor choice for video conferencing because they often ignore the accuracy of the recorded video and audio. Even the cheapest webcam will dramatically outperform those offers, allowing for a trouble-free conference. Ideally, you want to look at business solutions designed specifically for video conferencing and delivering superior performance in all aspects.

Webcam doesn't ask you to drop 250 dollars on the most expensive webcam you can find. Many webcams can deliver the professional quality of video that makes Zoom's high-definition and high-quality video quality shine. A 720p (1280 rb720) camera would be adequate for this. To stop choppy footage, get one under this resolution, which can produce at least 20 frames per second. If you want to invest the gas, get one that will shoot up to 30 frames per second.

Get a camera with highly sensitive autofocus and light correction capabilities to counter sudden movements and changes in lighting. It can be annoying to have to change your camera's focus manually, as participants watch your fingers fiddle around the lens.

INVEST IN GOOD QUALITY MICROPHONES

The type of microphone that you use will impact the ability of other participants to hear from you. Instead of the camera's built-in microphone, you can probably use a headset or clip-on microphone because you don't always remain close to the camera's microphone.

If you want people to understand you correctly, choose one that you can hold close to.

You should choose a microphone with an ample range of frequencies. If you buy an excellent microphone of studio-quality, get one with low impedance. 600 ohms (almost) or below is fine because it balances long cables without losing the quality of the audio. Make sure to check if the microphones are vulnerable to radio frequency interference (RFI) at all. You don't want a nearby cell phone during your meetings to generate deafening noises.

OTHER TIPS FOR ENHANCING THE AUDIO QUALITY

Audio efficiency is the most critical aspect of a Zoom meeting's overall performance. Here's how to get the best audio from a conference:

- While your laptop's webcam and built-in mic/speakers can work, a Bluetooth or wired (USB or headphone jack-style) headset can improve the call quality for better results. Or consider combining a Bluetooth speaker (an Amazon Echo or similar device may also use a Bluetooth speaker).

- When you join the Zoom call, you may need to switch your microphone and speaker option, no matter what method you choose. Once you have entered, pick your audio source by clicking on the arrow next to the audio / mute button.

- Mute to reduce background noise, to yourself or others.

- If you're like a coffee shop in a noisy location, just mute when you're not talking.

- If you are holding a conference, and the backgrounds of other participants are loud, tell them politely and ask them to mute or try to silence them.

- If your Internet connection isn't of high quality, you may find that the quality of the audio is suffering.

- Seek to disable video to protect your audio bandwidth over the internet.

- If you notice that your audio quality is starting to suffer, avoid downloading software or doing heavy web browsing too.

- If everything else fails, call in using a cell phone or a landline. You can stay connected to the video and screen sharing web conference.

GOOD LIGHTING IS IMPORTANT

Whatever the camera model you use, it's important to have good lighting. Poorly lighted spaces are the right way of hampering call quality and affecting your contact with others. Investing in just a few more powerful lights or merely rearranging your workspace is a cheap, easy way to improve the video conference quality without having to spend extra money or effort.

THE RIGHT POSTURE

Next are the finer details, such as keeping the proper posture. Slouching is out entirely, but the way you sit may impact the video conference quality. Try to maintain a stance that is upright but comfortable, which will provide excellent back support. Sitting in the wrong posture for a long period brings too much stress on the lower spine, leading to pain and back problems. Neither will make the conference enjoyable anymore.

MAKE EYE CONTACT

Human beings are social creatures, and one aspect of the intricate network of relationships is posture. A further issue is eye contact. In general, try to stay focused on the partner and aim your camera to make eye contact, or as close as possible to one. This will not only make you look focused and respectful but will also give the conversation a more professional, direct tone.

BANDWIDTH MANAGEMENT

Connectivity problems are a video conferencing epidemic, but most of them can be traced back to one thing: bandwidth. As stated by life hackers and numerous other websites, dial back bandwidth-intensive activities for optimal call quality. Evite downloads such as the plague, limit your visits to resource-intensive websites and try cutting back on multiplayer games for the duration of the conference. Shockingly, the connection is clogged with heavy server traffic.

CHAPTER 13:

Tips for Improving Your Internet Connection

In Zoom, the audio or video sometimes gets choppy or distorted. Use the best connection you can to the internet.

- Wired links are stronger than wireless communications (Wi-Fi, or cellular).

- Wi-Fi connections are better than cellular connections (3G/4G / LTE).

- Plan for Zoom meetings ahead and join Zoom meetings as often as possible from a place where you have a fast, reliable wired Internet connection.

- When you're not speaking, mute your microphone.

- Disable video on the HD Webcam.

- Webcam video broadcasting high definition (HD) requires more bandwidth than non-HD sending. Disabling HD video for other parts of your Zoom meeting will free up more of your Internet connection.

- Close your computer to other, unneeded applications.

- Meetings with zoomers will require considerable memory and processing power from your machine. Closing other applications during the session, which you don't need, will make Zoom run smoother.

- Large Uploads

- Big Uploads

- Cloud backups (e.g., CrashPlan, Carbonite)

- Synchronizations of cloud files (e.g., OneDrive, Dropbox);

- Other high bandwidth operations

- Communicate with your Zoom Meeting instructor or moderator.

- If a slow one, such as a weak cellular data connection, is the best Internet connection you have for Zoom, let the person or people running your session know in advance.

CHAPTER 14:

Zoom Myths

VIDEO CONFERENCING:

MYTH # 1: ALL VIDEO CONFERENCING SOFTWARE IS THE EXACT SAME

Zoom has a great deal going for it that nobody else does, like the sole real iOS and Android display sharing and the sole software-defined video conference room program, Zoom Rooms.

MYTH #2: YOU CAN NOT TRUST A START-UP

Zoom has been in existence for approximately five decades. They have secured healthy financing, thousands and thousands of consumers that, yes, cover, and an enthusiastic group that cares about offering the very best video communication solutions in the long term.

MYTH #3: CHEAP = CRAPPY

Quite often, you get exactly what you pay for. That amazing H&M $15 blazer? Yeah, that is likely to fall in two weeks. However, this is true with technology. Since technology is becoming much better and more scalable, Zoom is cheap for a reason, and the media is becoming cheaper. Honestly, what should be the price Zoom prices by video conferencing applications? You are getting gouged if you are paying more than this.

MYTH #4: ZOOM IS FOR DESKTOP CONFERENCING, I STILL WANT MY OLD SYSTEMS

Zoom is a portable computer and a desktop video. Would you like to maintain your seminar room strategies that are previous, by all means?

We've got a Cloud Room Connector which may work with almost any H.323 or SIP space system. However, we have conference space programs and our teleconferencing as part of our Zoom bundle. We could be your communications systems from the bottom up, not a fun adds on.

Perhaps you have blown your thoughts? Have you opened up to new methods of believing that you might have never envisioned?

If that's the case, you should register to get a live demonstration with a Zoom merchandise specialist!

VIDEO CONFERENCING MYTHS

The conferencing options are subject to lots of myths that were true at some point or another; this is logical. A number of them are still accurate for some providers.

MYTH #1: YOU WANT TONS OF BANDWIDTH FOR VIDEO

Odds are you watch YouTube frequently, even on 720p or 1080p resolutions. The World Wide Web is easily accessible and supplies a high quantity of bandwidth for streaming videos to spare. Nearly all internet connections can handle the crisp picture quality of Zoom. Even when a connection can't deal with the relatively modest quantity of bandwidth needed, Zoom mechanically lowers the video resolution for the player with bandwidth limitations so they can still take part, albeit using a slightly watered-down picture.

MYTH #2: VIDEO COMMUNICATION IS FOR BUSINESS BIG-WIGS. IT'S NO PLACE FOR A "MOM AND POP" ESTABLISHMENT

What about assistance and support? Clients appreciate it. The more you and your clients can connect, the more likely you are to achieve esteem and loyalty. It gives an experience that all companies should use within their ecosystems. Zoom is more than that, although sure, there are a few options that let you take part in a seminar. Across thousands of miles, you can collaborate with screen sharing. The ease of its interface does a fantastic job.

MYTH #3: IT IS EXPENSIVE

This is a line repeated about why they do not wish to try out Zoom. We cannot blame you. There are lots of solutions out there that drain you. Using Zoom, you do not have to look any farther. If you anticipate holding meetings with over two participants, then you just have to pay $9.99 a month for unlimited usage. It's free of charge! "What about hardware?" You may inquire. You are all set up if you have a microphone and a webcam

Myth #4: I Would Need to Hire An IT Crew?

Zoom does not ask that you have your infrastructure to be managed by IT staff. The Zoom team is prepared to support you each step along the way, making certain you're getting the best experience. Video conferencing should not want a degree in rocket science to install, and it does not.

MYTH #5: FIRMS CAN USE CONSUMER-BASED VIDEO PRODUCTS WITHOUT ANY ISSUES

The consumer marketplace has been different from the business-to-business (B2B) marketplace for a motive. One reason that companies opt to go for free consumer merchandise has to do with its low price and simplicity of use. However, Zoom manages this with the interface and its pricing. It behaves as consumer merchandise that is minimalistic while keeping each the qualities that companies use daily while focusing on getting out of the way so you can love using it. This can't be said about customer products.

CHAPTER 15:

50 Tips for How to Perform Your Best When Teaching Online

1. Guarantee Anxiety-Free Classroom; What do you know? Dread additionally represses learning results. Along these lines, never try to force fear by authorizing disciplines in your classroom. I have discovered that a few of us, the educators, are executing additional assignments as a discipline, because physical controls don't happen in showing today, as in the old and traditional period. Likewise, negative comments regularly offer ascent to fear among understudies in the

classroom. The dread in the classroom, regardless of whether it's for revenge or compromising remarks, will never motivate the students. In all actuality, dread is a hindrance to taking an interest effectively in the learning meeting. The understudy ought to never look to take a functioning part in the classroom. That is the reason each educator ought to keep up a dread free class to rouse the understudies. Along these lines, never offer negative expressions and troubling errands as disciplines.

2. Promote Their Ideas and Decisions; Advance imaginative learning in the classroom. Despite offering assignments and courses, allow them to choose the subject alone. Your learners will be motivated, for all things considered that they need to appreciate. Truly, thankfulness changes a great number of apprentices' lives. Your learners can't hold on to partake in your next talk. What's more, if you appreciate new thoughts, several incredible thoughts will likewise be presented to different apprentices in your homeroom. So consistently welcome new plans to motivate your apprentices.

3. Explain the Objective; Each learner enjoys clear guidelines. Explain every objective and target objective to be cultivated toward the start of the course. Remember to refer to the impediments they may look during the meeting. Examine potential cures about the difficulties they may confront. They will, subsequently, be propelled to address more issues, which will make the subject progressively available. Accordingly, you will find that your homeroom has become fruitful because

your understudies are empowered. As an instructor, you are setting up a nation, another world that will soon guide you and the earth."

4. Improve the Environment of the Classroom; Don't generally plunk down to talk about the exercise. Move next to the students and consider the experience. Keep them out of your group once in a while. Instruct them to visit the library now and again for investigation purposes. The move in the classroom condition animates the energy of the learning cerebrum, which is, truth be told, an essential for inspiration.

5. Be a Good Listener; Listen cautiously to what your understudy needs to state. Value their feelings and conclusions. Find a way to take care of the issues they talk about. Be an incredible audience, fellow. They will adore you when you hear them out with legitimate consideration. You will win their certainty, hence. Presently, is it difficult to move them? On the off chance that you need your understudies to hear you out, you need to hear them out first.

6. Share The Students' Experience; Not all apprentices can share their involvement with the course of the class. Some of them will be involved by understanding books. However, as sure learners examine their exercises related mastery, others might be motivated to take an interest effectively. Set up the exercise in such a rousing way, that different kinds of students can connect effectively in the sharing of exercises. In this circumstance, different learners are regularly propelled to

share their encounters. You can, subsequently, guarantee that the classroom is effective.

7. Positive Competition; The helpful rivalry is, fundamentally, a valuable system in the school. Guarantee the contention is productive. A decent contention in bunch work propels students hugely. We are additionally arranged to complete network work, which will likewise carry noteworthy advantages to their expert life. There is no uncertainty that sound rivalry sparkle energy among the learners in the classroom.

8. Know your Student Well; You have to realize your understudies well. You ought to likewise know their inclinations, their aversions, their viability, and their absence of execution. At the point when your understudies understand that you realize them well, they will start to like you and reveal their hindrances. This would be simpler for you to motivate your understudies correctly. You won't have the option to energize them since you realize them well.

9. Support Them and Give Them Responsibility; Give them the obligation of the apprentices. Allot them a class venture. They will then work with confidence. In such a circumstance, singular understudies may likewise need to satisfy their commitments. At the point when you give them obligations, trust inside themselves will develop, and they will start to feel that they are significant as they get an incentive from you. They would then be propelled to connect more in the

classroom. At the point when you confide in them, they will consistently confide in you consequently.

10. Show Your Enthusiasm; To convey your excitement in the classroom during a talk while meeting your obligations. Offer your energy about their extraordinary achievement. Once more, it shows an idealistic premium when each student presents another thought. Your demeanor of excitement will empower them.

11. Hold Your Record; Compose a report for you. Record each achievement of your learner. On the off chance that you locate that a particular understudy is changing, address the learner about change. Show the learner the record. Rewards and bolster the learner before the classroom. Indeed, even offer the progressions with your companions. On the off chance that an understudy finds that you're dealing with the learner while you address from your record, the learner is enlivened.

12. Valuable Feedback; On the off chance that an understudy isn't progressing nicely, incorporate positive input. At the point when important, offer another opportunity. Be a companion and look to comprehend the instance of such an awful outcome. Urge the understudy to rouse them to improve rapidly next time as he or she didn't see how to do well in this subject with legitimate information and procedure. Alright, guess what? Your valuable surveys will change a great number of lives. Take a gander best case scenario understudies in your school; you will get a lot of good

characteristics. Advise them regarding the delightful conditions they have. As a general rule, esteem them, which will rouse them altogether consequently.

13. Have an objective or schedule by Screen Sharing a paper or slide at the beginning of the course for each lesson. This adds up to students have a clear idea of how the class will proceed, what will be covered, and the tasks they will engage in.

14. Explore web behavior and student standards in the first simulated lesson, then refresh the topics daily.

15. Use a shared document in the Whiteboard or transcribe it, and let your learners also engage.

16. Where to share a Whiteboard, paper, screen, or photograph, seek math problems with whiteboarding, or let participants use annotation.

17. Identify items like grammar errors in a paper you share.

18. Taking the opportunity to progress the class questions, feedback, and responses. Give your users a minute to let them using answers, write in conversation, or be unmuted to ask any questions live.

19. Divide the conversation into smaller units on a given topic. You may use the Breakout Room feature in Zoom on pre-assign students to attend classes for a limited period so that they can address issues together.

20. Being the presenter, share the initiatives with the class. It helps the students to demonstrate what you are presenting.

21. Focus on student's delivery skills as they work. It also

encourages learners to hear from each other.

22. Pre-arrange the meeting and silence the microphones of the member upon entry. This helps to prevent background noise and allows for your students will focus on the class.

23. Aim at the monitor and get the students into eye touch. This tends to establish a more intimate link throughout teaching.

24. Take a second to test conversation or video of your students to check-in and receive input from the teachers.

25. Talk as though you are connected explicitly to the class while making sure you are at the proper distance to the microphone for excellent hearing performance.

26. Sharing photos, files, or videos while giving a presentation offer the students, a chance to loosen up or breathe in what you have shared.

27. Take a break after you stop debate and encourage the students to participate before moving further.

28. Give Invites in Advance – Meetings should not be a matter of the last minute. The invitations should go at least one day in advance of a structured conference.

29. Distribute the program – The program-less conference is simply a free-for-all. Create a plan and send it to the members so that they can address the subjects.

30. Provide Meeting Materials – When there are advance documents that need to be checked, ensure that they are presented as early as possible so that attendants can correctly interpret them.

31. Schedule Zoom Room – Make sure you arrange an appropriate meeting space that meets the number of participants and the meeting needed.

32. Set Meeting Goals – Maybe the most crucial thing you should do before the meeting scheduled is the objectives of, "What is the conference's mission?" The participants want to learn why they are participating in the meeting. This lays forth a reason for the conference. Be concise about the subject of the discussion.

33. Ensure your microphone gets muted when you are not talking. This minimizes any ambient noise or audio involvement. Use the Microphone button at the lower left of the Zoom menu that appears on the conference panel to silence the microphone. Additionally, you can configure your expectations for Zoom Meeting to automatically silence your microphone at the start of each meeting. Using the microphone button to unmute you, hold the enter key for as long as you are spoken. This simple rule provides for seamless operation of community meetings or discussions. Use noise cancellation software to improve the audio quality to the next stage for more appropriate ambient sound reduction. Muting your microphone can help in listening to lecture attentively and control sounds that can divert your attention.

34. Until capturing some audio or video conferencing, ensure all members in the meeting:

35. Ensure Meeting Settings before you Start a Meeting. Owing

to technological mishaps, it is highly reasonable for video conferences to be postponed or disrupted.

36. Turn on your computer to test whether Zoom is functioning correctly at least ten to fifteen minutes before each meeting

37. Sharing your screen helps meeting participants to understand your topic of presentation. When you are presenting or giving a lecture to your students, make sure you are sharing your screen with them. As an instructor, it will be beneficial for your learners to get an idea of the topic, and they will be able to take part in the discussion. It is not fascinating to attend lectures with voice only. Screen sharing will make speech more interesting, and you can watch any helpful video from YouTube or another website to support your topic.

38. Create a Meeting Agenda before you Schedule a Meeting. Team members are having difficulty participating efficiently if they do not know whether they should pay attention, give their feedback, or be part of the discussion process. If people assume they are involved in making decisions, but you want their feedback, the end of the discussion is likely to infuriate everyone. Updates are best allocated and perused before the conference, using a small section of the conference to address queries from the participants. If the aim is to make a judgment, state the rule governing the decision.

39. When you join the Zoom call, you may need to switch your microphone and speaker option, no matter what method you choose. Once you have entered, pick your audio source by

clicking on the arrow next to the audio/mute button.

40. Mute to reduce background noise, to yourself or others.

41. If you are like a coffee shop in a noisy location, just mute when you are not talking.

42. If you are holding a conference, and the backgrounds of other participants are loud, tell them politely and ask them to mute or try to silence them.

43. If your internet connection is not of high quality, you may find that the quality of the audio is suffering.

44. Seek to disable video to protect your audio bandwidth over the internet.

45. If you notice that your audio quality is starting to suffer, avoid downloading software or doing heavy web browsing too.

46. If everything else fails, call in using a cell phone or a landline. You can stay connected to the video and screen sharing web conference.

47. Hold brief video clips/lectures.

48. Sparingly use visuals, images, and animations when they can help to convey a point. • Keep text on a page or slide to a minimum when projecting text. Too much text or making text too small to fit on one slide will make it impossible to read in Zoom through screen sharing.

49. Use annotation tools from Zoom to point to specific information or direct student attention to a key point.

50. Build students directed or embedded questions or activities to do before or right after watching the video.

Conclusion

Technology has taken over most parts of the world and we humans are stuck to it as two magnets attached. We created technology many years ago for the sake of our ease, and over time, we have noticed that technology has helped us in our most difficult times. Technology has become the backbone of our modern society; without technology today, nothing seems to be possible.

Humans have reached the heights of success with the help of this technology. We can explore our universe while sitting in our homes. Life has become very easy and comfortable; thanks to our modern technology.

In this book, we have taken a long ride into the world of video conferencing with the help of the famous application Zoom. The Zoom app has helped us out through so many situations, and we cannot be more thankful to the inventor of the app. Today, we can regulate all our activities, schedules, different meetings, and conferences with the help of this amazing app.

The Zoom application has been under hot water due to some security concerns, but luckily the technical team of this application has been working tirelessly to make their clients feel comfortable sharing their documents, files, and other related stuff on the app. The app is being upgraded with a new version now and then to resolve the tiny issues that have been arising in the old versions. You are safe to use this app without the fear of being watched by someone else. There are various other video conferencing applications available, but why choose Zoom? Well, this question has also been answered in the book by comparing zoom to various other video conferencing apps. It is particularly clear that Zoom provides its clients with so many benefits and features that no other app can supply. You can use it for many purposes at any place and at any time.

Usually, many of us do not know the exact way to use a specific feature, and we consider the app useless; for such situations, we need to take command over an app. While talking about the Zoom app, there are certain tricks and tips that you can use to make this app work efficiently. Whether you are a host of the meeting or just the participant, you can use these tips and make your sessions more interesting and fun to attend.

The Zoom app has been popularly used in different fields, especially in schools, colleges, universities, and other teaching institutes. You can easily attend a class, sitting in your lounge, and make your learning times more relaxing than before. Many business meetings are held with the help of Zoom, especially multinational meetings in which people have to join from different regions of the world. Zoom has made life very easy for all individuals regardless of their fields and area of work. People have started to take their training sessions, yoga classes, attend religious ceremonies, and also attend weddings using this amazing app.

In short, life after the Zoom app has become exceptionally easy and convenient. Without being physically present, you can perform all your activities in the comfort of your home. So, it is time to download this amazing application onto your computer and mobile phone to have an extraordinary experience of virtual meetings and conferences without compromising on the quality.

CPSIA information can be obtained
at www.ICGtesting.com
Printed in the USA
BVHW041344280921
617682BV00019B/524